OFFICIAL TOUR

Stay by the Beach

Information at your fingertips

This pocket guide is aimed at holidaymakers looking for quality-rated accommodation near an award-winning beach in England. You will find a selection of hotels, B&Bs, self-catering holiday homes and camping/caravan parks that are within 2.5 miles of an award-winning beach. The beaches in this guide held an award at the time of going to print.

Star ratings

Establishments are awarded a rating of one to five stars based on a combination of quality of facilities and services provided. The more stars, the higher the quality and the greater the range of facilities and level of service.

The process to arrive at a star rating is very thorough to ensure that when you book accommodation you can be confident it will meet your expectations. Enjoy England professional assessors visit establishments annually and work to strict criteria to rate the available facilities and service.

A quality score is awarded for every aspect of the experience. For hotels and B&B accommodation this includes the comfort of the bed, the quality of the breakfast and dinner and, most importantly, the cleanliness. For self-catering properties the assessors also take into consideration the layout and design of the accommodation, the ease of use of all appliances, the range and quality of the kitchen equipment, and the variety and presentation of the visitor information provided. The warmth of welcome and the level of care that each establishment offers its guests are noted, and places that go the extra mile to make every stay a special one will be rewarded with high scores for quality.

All the national assessing bodies (VisitBritain, VisitScotland, Visit Wales and the AA*) now operate to a common set of standards for rating each category of accommodation, giving holidaymakers and travellers a clear guide on exactly what to expect at each level. An explanation of the star ratings is given below:

Ratings made easy

★	Simple, practical, no frills
★★	Well presented and well run
★★★	Good level of quality and comfort
★★★★	Excellent standard throughout
★★★★★	Exceptional with a degree of luxury

For full details of Enjoy England's Quality assessment schemes go online at **enjoyengland.com/quality**

Awaiting confirmation of rating

At the time of going to press some establishments featured in this guide had not yet been assessed for their rating for the year 2007 and so their new rating could not be included. Rating Applied For indicates this.

** The AA does not assess self-catering properties.*

Gold and Silver Awards

The Enjoy England awards are highly prized by proprietors and are only given to hotels and bed and breakfast accommodation offering the highest level of quality within their star rating, particularly in areas of housekeeping, service and hospitality, bedrooms, bathrooms and food.

National Accessible Scheme

Establishments with a National Accessible Scheme rating provide access and facilities for guests with special visual, hearing and mobility needs.

Designators explained

Hotel	A minimum of six bedrooms, but more likely to have more than 20.
Small Hotel	A maximum of 20 bedrooms and likely to be more personally run.
Guest Accommodation	Encompassing a wide range of establishments from one room B&Bs to larger properties which may offer dinner and hold an alcohol licence.
B&B	Accommodating no more than six people, the owners of these establishments welcome you into their own home as a special guest.
Guesthouse	Generally comprising more than three rooms. Dinner is unlikely to be available (if it is, it will need to be booked in advance). May be licensed.
Farm	B&B, and sometimes dinner, but always on a farm.
Restaurant with Rooms	A licensed restaurant is the main business but there will be a small number of bedrooms, with all the facilities you would expect, and breakfast the following morning.
Inn	Pub with rooms, and many with restaurants, too.
Self Catering	Chose from cosy country cottages, smart town-centre apartments, seaside villas, grand country houses for large family gatherings, and even quirky conversions of windmills, railway carriages and lighthouses. Most take bookings by the week, generally from a Friday or Saturday, but short breaks are increasingly offered, particularly outside the main season.
Hostel	Safe, budget-priced, short-term accommodation for individuals and groups.
Camping Park*	These sites only have pitches available for tents.
Touring Park*	If you are planning to travel with your own caravan, motor home or tent, then look out for a Touring Park.
Holiday Park*	If you want to hire a caravan holiday home for a short break or longer holiday, or are looking to buy your own holiday home, a Holiday Park is the right choice. They range from small, rural sites to large parks with all the added extras such as a pool.

* Many parks will offer a combination of these designators

How to use this guide

Each accommodation entry contains information that proprietors provide regional tourist partners (except for ratings and awards).

1 2 3 4 5

STRETE – BLACKPOOL SANDS

Strete Barton Farmhouse ★★★★Guest Accommodation
Totnes Road, Strete, Dartmouth, Devon TQ6 0RN SILVER AWARD

T:	+44 (0) 1803 770364
E:	david@stretebarton.co.uk
W:	stretebarton.co.uk
Bedrooms:	6 • £65.00-£85.00 per double room per night, breakfast included • Debit/credit card; cheques/cash accepted
Open:	Year round except Christmas
Description:	16thC farmhouse with stunning sea views. Six exquisitely furnished bedrooms either en suite or private facilities. English or continental breakfast.
Facilities:	✕P
Facilities:	1.05 miles

CYCLISTS WELCOME WALKERS WELCOME

6 7 8 9 10

1	Postal town
2	Establishment name
3	Establishment address (or booking address if self catering)
4	Enjoy England Quality Rose star rating and designator
5	Gold or Silver Award where applicable
6	Telephone, email and website address – note that web addresses are shown without the prefix www.
7	Accommodation details, prices and details of when establishment is open
8	At-a-glance facility symbols (for key see facing page)
9	Accessible rating where applicable
10	Cyclists/Walkers Welcome where applicable

Please note that sample entry is for illustration purposes only.
Not all symbols shown will apply to this establishment.

Key to symbols

Rooms

- Non-smoking rooms available
- Microwave
- Radio
- Tea/coffee facilities in all bedrooms
- Phone in all bedrooms
- Central heating
- Colour TV
- Video player
- DVD player
- Four-poster bed available
- Freezer
- Hairdryer in all bedrooms

General

- Non-smoking establishment
- Night porter
- Parking on site
- Public phone
- Open fires
- Restaurant
- Evening entertainment
- Pets welcome
- Washing machine or laundry facilities
- Ironing facilities
- Shower on site
- Motor home waste disposal point
- Overnight holding area
- Drinking water supply

Leisure

- Sauna
- Swimming pool – outdoor
- Swimming pool – indoor
- Riding/pony trekking nearby
- Tennis court(s)
- Games room
- Fishing nearby
- Golf nearby
- Gym/fitness room

Mobility Symbols

Typically suitable for a person with sufficient mobility to climb a flight of steps but who would benefit from fixtures and fittings to aid balance.

Typically suitable for a person with restricted walking ability and for those who may need to use a wheelchair some of the time and can negotiate a maximum of three steps.

Typically suitable for a person who depends on the use of a wheelchair and transfers to and from the wheelchair in a seated position. This person may be an independent traveller.

Typically suitable for a person who depends on the use of a wheelchair in a seated position. This person also requires personal/ mechanical assistance to aid transfer (eg carer, hoist).

Visual Impairment Symbols

Typically provides key additional services and facilities to meet the needs of visually impaired guests.

Typically provides a higher level of additional services and facilities to meet the needs of visually impaired guests.

Hearing Impairment Symbols

Typically provides key additional services and facilities to meet the needs of guests with a hearing impairment.

Typically provides a higher level of additional services and facilities to meet the needs of guests with a hearing impairment.

Cyclists Welcome and Walkers Welcome

Participants actively encourage cycling and walking by providing clean up areas for washing or drying off, help with special meal arrangements, maps and books to look up for cycling and walking routes.

CARBIS BAY

Carbis Bay Hotel ★★★Hotel

Carbis Bay, St Ives, TR26 2NP

T:	+44 (0) 1736 795311
E:	carbisbayhotel@talk21.com
W:	carbisbayhotel.co.uk
Bedrooms:	38 • £102.00-£182.00 per double room per night, breakfast included • Debit/credit card accepted
Open:	Year round
Description:	Award-winning hotel set in its own grounds overlooking its own beach. AA rosetted restaurant with superb choice of menu and wine. Beachside self-catering houses also available. Heated, outdoor swimming pool, sun terrace, games room, all bedrooms are en suite.
Facilities:	◐P⛳🐕
To Beach:	0.09 miles

CONSTANTINE BAY

Trevose Golf & Country Club ★★/★★Self Catering

Constantine Bay, Padstow, Cornwall, PL28 8JB

T:	+44 (0) 1841 520208
E:	info@trevose-gc.co.uk
W:	trevose-gc.co.uk
Units:	31 • £53.00-£910.00 per unit per week • Debit/credit card accepted
Open:	Year round
Description:	Trevose Golf & Country Club is on one of the most beautiful stretches of the North Coast of Cornwall. Trevose offers an ideal holiday for either real golfing enthusiasts or for others who wish to play golf on occasion and enjoy the beaches.
Facilities:	P⛳
To Beach:	0.5 miles

CRANTOCK – FISTRAL BEACH

Fairbank Hotel ★★Small Hotel

West Pentire Road, Crantock, Newquay, TR8 5SA

T:	+44 (0) 1637 830424
E:	enquiries@fairbankhotel.co.uk
W:	fairbankhotel.co.uk
Bedrooms:	14 • £70.00-£80.00 per double room per night, breakfast included • Debit/credit card accepted
Open:	Year round
Description:	Sit back, relax and enjoy the view. From the moment you arrive, your hosts will do their utmost to ensure that you have a happy and enjoyable stay.
Facilities:	P🐕
To Beach:	1.01 miles

GOLDENBANK – GYLLYNGVASE BEACH

Pendra Loweth Holiday Cottages ★★★★Self Catering

Maen Valley, Falmouth, Cornwall, TR11 5BJ

T:	+44 (0) 1326 312190
E:	pendraloweth@aol.com
W:	pendra.co.uk
Units:	82 • Up to £730.00 per unit per week – call for details • Debit/credit card accepted
Open:	Year round
Description:	Holiday Cottages situated in a beautiful sheltered south-facing, wooded valley. One mile from beaches and two miles from Falmouth. Cottages for hire. There is a shop, cafe bar, laundry and tennis. Family-run with families in mind.
Facilities:	P✕
To Beach:	1.25 miles

MULLION – THE TOWANS

Polurrian Hotel ★★★Hotel

Polurrian Hotel Polurrian Road, Mullion, Helston, TR12 7EN

T:	+44 (0) 1326 240421
E:	relax@polurrianhotel.com
W:	polurrianhotel.com
Bedrooms:	39 • £106.00-£198.00 per double room per night, breakfast included • Debit/credit card accepted
Open:	Year round
Description:	Polurrian Hotel is set in its own grounds above a sandy cove. It boasts Edwardian elegance amid scenic splendour. Long- or short-stays and families welcomed.
Facilities:	P
To Beach:	1.33 miles

MULLION – THE TOWANS

Trenance Farm Cottages ★★★Self Catering

Mullion, Helston, Cornwall, TR12 7HB

T:	+44 (0) 1326 240639
E:	info@trenancefarmholidays.co.uk
W:	trenancefarmholidays.co.uk
Units:	9 • £190.00-£709.00 per unit per week • Debit/credit card accepted
Open:	Year round
Description:	Very comfortable two-/three-bedroomed cottages, converted from old stone buildings, all with their own gardens. The owners invite you to come and relax in the mature gardens and listen to the wildlife or enjoy swimming in the heated, outdoor pool. Two games rooms also available.
Facilities:	P
To Beach:	1.46 miles

NEWQUAY – FISTRAL BEACH

Esplanade Hotel

★★★Hotel

9 Esplanade Road, Newquay, Cornwall, TR7 1PS

T:	+44 (0) 1637 873333
E:	info@newquay-hotels.co.uk
W:	newquay-hotels.co.uk
Bedrooms:	103 • £50.00-£120.00 per double room per night, breakfast included • Debit/credit card accepted
Open:	Year round
Description:	A warm welcome awaits you at the Esplanade Hotel, a modern establishment directly overlooking the magnificent Fistral Beach. A wide range of facilities are available including, indoor and outdoor pools, sauna, spa and solarium.
Facilities:	[icons]
To Beach:	0.07 miles

NEWQUAY – PORTH BEACH

Whipsiderry Hotel

★★Hotel
SILVER AWARD

Trevelgue Road, Porth, Newquay, Cornwall, TR7 3LY

T:	+44 (0) 1637 874777
E:	info@whipsiderry.co.uk
W:	whipsiderry.co.uk
Bedrooms:	23 • £90.00-£114.00 per double room per night, breakfast included • Debit/credit card accepted
Open:	Year round
Description:	The Whipsiderry Hotel offers breathtaking views over Porth Beach and bay. Standing in approximately 2.5 acres of its own grounds it has 23 well-appointed bedrooms – all with modern amenities, some at ground level.
Facilities:	[icons]
To Beach:	0.13 miles

ROCK – POLZEATH BEACH

St Enodoc Hotel

★★★Hotel
SILVER AWARD

Rock, Wadebridge, Cornwall, PL27 6LA

T:	+44 (0) 1208 863394
E:	enodochotel@aol.com
W:	enodoc-hotel.co.uk
Bedrooms:	20 • £100.00-£345.00 per double room per night, breakfast included • Debit/credit card accepted
Open:	Year round
Description:	The St Enodoc Hotel provides a distinctive style and relaxed atmosphere. As well as being the ideal location for your summer holiday with its heated, outdoor pool and adjoining golf courses, the hotel is the perfect retreat.
Facilities:	[icons]
To Beach:	1.93 miles

ROCK – POLZEATH BEACH

Tzitzikama Lodge ★★★★Guest Accommodation

Rock Road, Rock, Padstow, Cornwall, PL27 6NP

T: +44 (0) 1208 862839
E: tzitzikama.lodge@btinternet.com
W: cornwall-online.co.uk/tzitzikama-lodge

Bedrooms: 3 • £62.00-£70.00 per double room per night, breakfast included • Debit/credit card accepted

Open: Year round

Description: Stylish, comfortable, en suite bedrooms with tea-/coffee-making facilities, TVs and cleaning service. Continental or full English breakfasts available from the menu.

Facilities:

To Beach: 1.84 miles

ST IVES – PORTHMEOR BEACH

Monterey ♦♦♦♦Guest Accommodation

7 Clodgy View, St Ives, Cornwall, TR26 1JG

T: +44 (0) 1736 794248
E: info@monterey-stives.fsnet.co.uk
W: monterey-stives.co.uk

Bedrooms: 5 • £50.00-£65.00 per double room per night, breakfast included • Debit/credit card; cheques/cash accepted

Open: Year round except Christmas and New Year

Description: Friendly, comfortable guesthouse offering excellent breakfasts. Stunning sea views await visitors. Five minutes to wonderful, sandy beach, galleries, harbour and town centre.

Facilities:

To Beach: 0.19 miles

ST IVES – PORTHMEOR BEACH

Pierview ♦♦♦♦Guest Accommodation

32-34 Back Road East, St Ives, Cornwall, TR26 1PD

T: +44 (0) 1736 794268
E: pierviewstives@aol.com
W: pierview-stives.co.uk

Bedrooms: 7 • £55.00-£70.00 per double room per night, breakfast included • Debit/credit card; cheques/cash accepted

Open: Year round

Description: Pierview was originally two fisherman's cottages in the Downalong quarter of old St Ives. The properties have been tastefully converted while retaining their original characteristics and outward charm.

Facilities:

To Beach: 0.21 miles

ST IVES – PORTHMEOR BEACH

Tregony Guesthouse ♦♦♦♦Guest Accommodation

1 Clodgy View, St Ives, Cornwall, TR26 1JG SILVER AWARD

T:	+44 (0) 1736 795884
E:	val@tregony.com
W:	tregony.com
Bedrooms:	5 • £56.00-£70.00 per double room per night, breakfast included • Debit/credit card accepted
Open:	Year round
Description:	A warm, friendly atmosphere awaits you at Tregony, where the sole aim is to ensure that your holiday is both happy and memorable. Overlooking Porthmeor Beach, with beautiful views of Clodgy Point and The Island.
Facilities:	
To Beach:	0.16 miles

ST IVES – PORTHMINSTER BEACH

Carlyon Guesthouse ★★★Guesthouse

The Terrace, St Ives, Cornwall, TR26 2BP

T:	+44 (0) 1736 795317
E:	andrea.papworth@btinternet.com
W:	carlyon-stives.co.uk
Bedrooms:	6 • £50.00-£60.00 per double room per night, breakfast included
Open:	Year round
Description:	The Carlyon is a family-run business found above the award-winning Porthminster Beach. Most rooms have stunning sea, beach and coastal views. It is a three-minute walk to the town and shops; two minutes to the beach.
Facilities:	P
To Beach:	0.17 miles

ST MAWGAN – BEACON COVE

Dalswinton House ★★★★Guest Accommodation

St Mawgan-in-Pydar, Newquay, Cornwall, TR8 4EZ

T:	+44 (0) 1637 860385
E:	dalswinton@bigwig.net
W:	dalswinton.com
Bedrooms:	8 • £70.00 per double room per night, breakfast included • Debit/credit card accepted
Open:	Year round
Description:	Approached along its own private drive, Dalswinton House is a Victorian slate- and stone-built former farmhouse of character that was privately occupied until the late 1960s. It stands in eight acres of secluded, south-facing grounds.
Facilities:	P
To Beach:	1.96 miles

ST MINVER – POLZEATH BEACH

The Farmhouse ★★★★Self Catering

Booking: Rock Holidays inc. Harbour Holidays Rock, Trebetherick House, PL27 6SB

T: +44 (0) 1208 863399
E: rockhols@aol.com
W: rockholidays.co.uk

Units: 1 • £700.00-£2,300.00 per unit per week • Debit/credit card accepted

Open: Year round

Description: A beautifully restored 17thC farmhouse beside the lake at Roserrow and only yards from a golf course and facilities. The accommodation is very spacious with a huge kitchen, which has an Aga and large dining table that can seat 12.

Facilities:

To Beach: 1.04 miles

TINTAGEL – TREBARWITH STRAND

Pendrin Guesthouse ♦♦♦♦Guest Accommodation

Atlantic Road, Tintagel, Cornwall, PL34 0DE

T: +44 (0) 1840 770560
E: pendrin@tesco.net
W: pendrinhouse.co.uk

Bedrooms: 9 • £56.00-£62.00 per double room per night, breakfast included • Debit/credit card accepted

Open: February to November

Description: A beautiful, warm and welcoming Victorian house overlooking the cliffs and the Atlantic Ocean in the historic village of Tintagel. Close to the castle, coastal path and many amenities.

Facilities: P

To Beach: 1.43 miles

WATERGATE BAY – BEACON COVE

Tregurrian Hotel ★ Hotel

Watergate Bay, Newquay, Cornwall, TR8 4AB

T: +44 (0) 1637 860280
E: tregurrianhotel@breaksincornwall.com
W: tregurrianhotel.com

Bedrooms: 30 • Up to £74.00 per double room per night, breakfast included – call for details • Debit/credit card accepted

Open: Year round

Description: Just 100 yards from spectacular Atlantic coastline and superb sandy beach this well-appointed, value-for-money hotel offers a friendly welcome in a relaxed and informal atmosphere. Amenities include attractive bar, sun lounge and conservatory.

Facilities: P

To Beach: 1.04 miles

CUMBRIA

MILLOM – HAVERIGG BEACH

Duddon Estuary YHA ★★★Hostel

Borwick Rails, Millom, Cumbria, LA18 4JU

T: +44 (0) 1229 773937
E: duddon@yha.org.uk
W: duddonyha.org.uk

Dormitories: 18 • £10.00-£12.00 per person per night, room only • Debit/credit card accepted

Open: Year round

Description: Hostel accommodation in a peaceful location with superb views. Suitable for families, groups and individuals. Also accessible for those with disabilities. Great location for bird-watching, cycling, walking and fishing.

Facilities:

To Beach: 1.7 miles

SILLOTH – SILLOTH WEST BEACH

Stanwix Park Holiday Centre ★★★★★Holiday, Touring & Caravan Park

Greenrow, Silloth, Cumbria, CA7 4HH — ROSE AWARD

T: +44 (0) 1697 332666
E: enquiries@stanwix.com
W: stanwix.com

Pitches: 123 • £16.80-£20.50 per caravan per night • Debit/credit card accepted

Open: Year round

Description: Caravan holiday homes for hire. Large leisure centre. Pools, ten-pin bowling and amusement arcade, family entertainment, disco and adult cabaret. Situated on the Solway Coast, a popular base from which to explore the Lake District.

Facilities: P

To Beach: 0.43 miles

DEVON

BERRYNARBOR – COMBE MARTIN BEACH

Langleigh Guesthouse ★★★★Guest Accommodation

The Village, Berrynarbor, Ilfracombe, Devon, EX34 9SG

T: +44 (0) 1271 883410
E: relax@langleighguesthouse.co.uk
W: langleighguesthouse.co.uk

Bedrooms: 6 • £50.00-£55.00 per double room per night, breakfast included • Debit/credit card; cheques/cash accepted

Open: Year round

Description: Family-run guesthouse where all the food is home-cooked. It offers relaxation and beautiful views of the countryside.

Facilities: P

To Beach: 1.05 miles

BERRYNARBOR – COMBE MARTIN BEACH

Sandaway Beach Holiday Park ★★★★Holiday Park

Berrynarbor, Ilfracombe, Devon, EX34 9ST ROSE AWARD

T: +44 (0) 1271 866766
E: stay@johnfowlerholidays.com
W: johnfowlerholidays.com

Pitches: 134 • £14.00-£33.00 per caravan per night • Debit/credit card; cheques/cash accepted

Open: Seasonal opening – contact for details

Description: Well designed, laid out site which is carefully screened. Overlooking the sea and close to own beach.

Facilities:

To Beach: 0.31 miles

BERRYNARBOR – COMBE MARTIN BEACH

The Lodge ♦♦♦♦Guest Accommodation

Pitt Hill, Ilfracombe, Devon, EX34 9SG

T: +44 (0) 1271 883246
E: philbridle@aol.com
W: lodge-country-house-hotel.co.uk

Bedrooms: 6 • £50.00-£56.00 per double room per night, breakfast included • Debit/credit card; cheques/cash accepted

Open: Year round except Christmas

Description: Family-run hotel with large garden and car park. It's friendly, comfortable and all bedrooms are equipped with colour TV and tea-/coffee-making facilities.

Facilities: TV

To Beach: 1.05 miles

BIDEFORD – WESTWARD HO!

The Mount ★★★★Guesthouse

Northdown Road, Bideford, Devon, EX39 3LP

T: +44 (0) 1237 473748
E: andrew@themountBideford.fsnet.co.uk
W: themount1.cjb.net

Bedrooms: 8 • £56.00-£62.00 per double room per night, breakfast included • Debit/credit card; cheques/cash accepted

Open: Year round except Christmas

Description: Small, family-run Georgian guesthouse with character and charm. A non-smoking establishment which is a short walk to town centre and quay. All rooms en suite with TVs.

Facilities: TV

To Beach: 1.84 miles

BIGBURY ON SEA

The Henley Hotel

★★Small Hotel
SILVER AWARD

Folly Hill, Bigbury on Sea, Kingsbridge, Devon, TQ7 4AR

T: +44 (0) 1548 810240
E: enquiries@thehenleyhotel.co.uk
W: thehenleyhotel.co.uk

Bedrooms: 6 • £90.00-£120.00 per double room per night, breakfast included • Debit/credit card; cheques/cash accepted

Open: Seasonal opening – call for details

Description: Edwardian, cottage-style hotel with spectacular sea views. Private steps through garden lead to an to excellent beach. Good walking and golf nearby.

Facilities:

To Beach: 0.37 miles

BISHOPSTEIGNTON – NESS COVE

Whidborne Manor

♦♦♦♦Guest Accommodation
SILVER AWARD

Ash Hill, Bishopsteignton, Teignmouth, Devon, TQ14 9PY

T: +44 (0) 1626 870177
E: nicola.dykes@ntlworld.com
W: whidbornemanor.co.uk

Bedrooms: 3 • £40.00-£50.00 per double room per night, breakfast included

Open: Seasonal opening – call for details

Description: 15thC thatched Devon Longhouse set in peaceful location but close to the coast. Whidborne Manor offers comfortable accommodation in a family environment.

Facilities:

To Beach: 1.89 miles

BRIXHAM – ST MARY'S BAY

Anchorage Guesthouse

★★★★Guesthouse

170 New Road, Brixham, Devon, TQ5 8DA

T: +44 (0) 1803 852960
E: enquiries@Brixham-anchorage.co.uk
W: Brixham-anchorage.co.uk

Bedrooms: 8 • £36.00-£50.00 per double room per night, breakfast included • Debit/credit card accepted

Open: Year round except Christmas and New Year

Description: Bungalow guesthouse offering mainly en suite rooms. Situated in a level position with ample off-road car parking.

Facilities: P

To Beach: 0.97 miles

BRIXHAM – ST MARY'S BAY

Sea Tang Guesthouse ★★★★Guesthouse

67 Berry Head Road, Brixham, Devon, TQ5 9AA

T: +44 (0) 1803 854651
E: seatangguesthouse@yahoo.co.uk
W: smoothhound.co.uk/hotels/seatang.html

Bedrooms: 6 • £43.00-£49.00 per double room per night, breakfast included

Open: Year round except Christmas and New Year

Description: Sea Tang is a non-smoking establishment with six en suite bedrooms that enjoy magnificent views across the marina and Torbay.

Facilities:

To Beach: 0.5 miles

CHURSTON FERRERS – GOODRINGTON SOUTH SANDS

White Horse Hotel ★★★★Guest Accommodation

Dartmouth Road, Churston Ferrers, Brixham, Devon, TQ5 0LL

T: +44 (0) 1803 842381
E: bookings@thewhitehorsehotel.co.uk
W: thewhitehorsehotel.co.uk

Bedrooms: 8 • £50.00-£56.00 per double room per night, breakfast included • Debit/credit card accepted

Open: Year round except New Year

Description: Family-run, licensed guesthouse with all rooms en suite. It is just minutes' walk from the beach and adjacent to Devon Steam Railway.

Facilities:

To Beach: 1.97 miles

COMBE MARTIN

Blair Lodge Hotel ♦♦♦Guest Accommodation

Moory Meadow, Seaview, Combe Martin, Ilfracombe, Devon, EX34 0DG

T: +44 (0) 1271 882294
E: info@blairlodge.co.uk
W: blairlodge.co.uk

Bedrooms: 9 • £50.00-£52.00 per double room per night, breakfast included • Debit/credit card accepted

Open: Year round

Description: Superb, licensed, private hotel in a quiet location on the edge of Exmoor, overlooking Combe Martin Bay. Excellent reputation for high standards and good value.

Facilities:

To Beach: 0.18 miles

COMBE MARTIN

Channel Vista ♦♦♦♦Guest Accommodation

Woodlands, Combe Martin, Ilfracombe, Devon, EX34 0AT

T:	+44 (0) 1271 883514
E:	channelvista@freeuk.com
W:	channelvista.aonesites.co.uk
Bedrooms:	6 • £46.00-£50.00 per double room per night, breakfast included • Debit/credit card accepted
Open:	Year round except New Year
Description:	Charming, Victorian residence completed to high standard. All rooms fully en suite. Private, on-site parking. Licensed bar and excellent cuisine.
Facilities:	[icons]
To Beach:	0.08 miles

COMBE MARTIN

Mellstock House ♦♦♦♦Guest Accommodation

Woodlands, Combe Martin, Devon, EX34 0AR

T:	+44 (0) 1271 882592
E:	mary@mellstockhouse.co.uk
W:	mellstockhouse.co.uk
Bedrooms:	6 • £47.00-£52.00 per double room per night, breakfast included • Debit/credit card accepted
Open:	Year round except Christmas
Description:	Family-run, Edwardian, licensed guesthouse. Sea and country views. All rooms en suite. Close to Exmoor and just two minutes to sea.
Facilities:	[icons]
To Beach:	0.06 miles

COMBE MARTIN

Saffron House Hotel ★★★Guest Accommodation

King Street, Combe Martin, Ilfracombe, Devon, EX34 0BX

T:	+44 (0) 1271 883521
E:	stay@saffronhousehotel.co.uk
W:	saffronhousehotel.co.uk
Bedrooms:	9 • £42.00-£46.00 per double room per night, breakfast included • Debit/credit card accepted
Open:	Seasonal opening – call for details
Description:	Charming 17thC hotel close to beaches and Exmoor. Well-appointed en suite rooms with colour TV. There is a lounge bar, log fires and heated pool. Children welcome.
Facilities:	[icons]
To Beach:	0.33 miles

CROYDE – CROYDE BAY

Moorsands ♦♦♦Guest Accommodation

34 Moor Lane, Croyde Bay, Braunton, Devon, EX33 1NP

T: +44 (0) 1271 890781
E: paul@moorsands.co.uk
W: croyde-bay.com/moorsands.htm

Bedrooms: 4 • £52.00-£64.00 per double room per night, breakfast included

Open: Year round except Christmas

Description: Former Victorian hotel with stunning views. Short walks to beach or village. This small establishment offers comfortable, spacious rooms, a warm welcome and delicious breakfasts.

Facilities:

To Beach: 0.33 miles

DAWLISH – CORYTON COVE

Channel View Guesthouse ♦♦♦Guest Accommodation

14 Teignmouth Hill, West Cliff, Dawlish, Devon, EX7 9DN

T: +44 (0) 1626 866973
E: channelviewguesthouse@fsmail.net
W: channelviewguesthouse.co.uk

Bedrooms: 3 • £45.00-£55.00 per double room per night, breakfast included

Open: Seasonal opening – call for details

Description: Beautiful period house with lovely sea views from most rooms. It has been upgraded to the highest standards and is only a few minutes' walk from the beach, lawn and stream as well as shops, railway and bus station.

Facilities:

To Beach: 0.22 miles

DAWLISH – DAWLISH WARREN BEACH

Leadstone Camping ★★★Camping & Touring Park

Warren Road, Dawlish, Devon, EX7 0NG

T: +44 (0) 1626 864411
E: info@leadstonecamping.co.uk
W: leadstonecamping.co.uk

Pitches: 245 • £13.90-£15.55 per caravan per night • Debit/credit card; cheques/cash accepted

Open: Seasonal opening – call for details

Description: Friendly, quiet, uncommercialised site set amid rolling grassland in a natural, secluded bowl. Close to Dawlish Warren's two-mile beach of golden sands and dunes.

Facilities:

To Beach: 0.74 miles

EXMOUTH – DAWLISH WARREN BEACH

New Moorings ★★★★Guest Accommodation

1 Morton Road, Exmouth, Devon, EX8 1AZ

T: +44 (0) 1395 223073
E: anneanddave@newmoorings.wanadoo.co.uk
W: exmouthguide.co.uk/newmoorings.htm

Bedrooms: 6 • £52.00-£54.00 per double room per night, breakfast included • Debit/credit card; cheques/cash accepted

Open: Year round except Christmas

Description: This is a comfortable, welcoming, non-smoking establishment where all rooms are en suite. Close to the seafront, town centre, marina and train/bus stations.

Facilities:

To Beach: 1.48 miles

EXMOUTH – DAWLISH WARREN BEACH

The Swallows ★★★★Guest Accommodation

11 Carlton Hill, Exmouth, Devon, EX8 2AJ

T: +44 (0) 1395 263937
E: p.russo@btclick.com
W: exmouth-guide.co.uk/swallows.htm

Bedrooms: 5 • £52.00-£56.00 per double room per night, breakfast included • Debit/credit card accepted

Open: Year round except New Year

Description: Late Georgian townhouse, standing 300 yards from seafront and town centre, providing comfortable and friendly guest accommodation.

Facilities:

To Beach: 1.67 miles

GALMPTON – HOPE COVE

Burton Farmhouse & Garden Restaurant ★★★★Farm

Galmpton, Kingsbridge, Devon, TQ7 3EY

T: +44 (0) 1548 561210
E: anne@burtonfarm.co.uk
W: burtonfarm.co.uk

Bedrooms: 15 • £65.00-£75.00 per double room per night, breakfast included • Debit/credit card; cheques/cash accepted

Open: Year round except Christmas and New Year

Description: Beautifully restored 400-year-old farmhouse. A little more than a mile from Hope Cove, along a private road, surrounded by fields and farms.

Facilities:

To Beach: 1.12 miles

HILLHEAD – ST MARY'S BAY

Raddicombe Lodge ★★★★Guest Accommodation

Kingswear Road, Brixham, Devon, TQ5 0EX

T:	+44 (0) 1803 882125
E:	stay@raddicombelodge.co.uk
W:	raddicombelodge.co.uk
Bedrooms:	9 • £47.00-£56.00 per double room per night, breakfast included • Debit/credit card; cheques/cash accepted
Open:	Year round except Christmas and New Year
Description:	Luxury accommodation with nine en suite guestrooms affording sea and country views. Delicious food at this non-smoking lodge. Private car park. Close to beaches and walks.
Facilities:	
To Beach:	1.98 miles

HOLCOMBE – CORYTON COVE

Manor Farm ♦♦♦♦Guest Accommodation

Holcombe Village, Holcombe, Dawlish, Devon, EX7 0JT

T:	+44 (0) 1626 863020
E:	humphreyclem@aol.com
W:	farmaccom.com
Bedrooms:	3 • £42.00-£48.00 per double room per night, breakfast included • Cheques/cash accepted
Open:	Year round except Christmas and New Year
Description:	Peaceful, Victorian farmhouse on a working farm in a pretty village between Dawlish and Teignmouth. It offers a warm welcome – and farmhouse breakfast is a speciality. It also boasts a lounge, garden, snooker table and sea views.
Facilities:	
To Beach:	0.93 miles

HOPE COVE

Cottage Hotel ★★★Guest Accommodation

Hope Cove, Kingsbridge, Devon, TQ7 3HJ

T:	+44 (0) 1548 561555
E:	info@hopecove.com
W:	hopecove.com
Bedrooms:	35 • £32.00-£57.50 per double room per night, breakfast included • Debit/credit card; cheques/cash accepted
Open:	Seasonal opening – call for details
Description:	Set in two acres of grounds in a secluded South Devon fishing village, Cottage Hotel has spectacular views as it overlooks Bolt Tail and Bigbury Bay.
Facilities:	
To Beach:	0.07 miles

ILFRACOMBE – HELE BEACH

Hele Valley Holiday Park

★★★★Holiday, Touring & Camping Park

Hele Bay, Ilfracombe, Devon, EX34 9RD

T: +44 (0) 1271 862460
E: holidays@helevalley.co.uk
W: helevalley.co.uk

Pitches: 90 • £13.00-£19.00 per motor caravan per night • Debit/credit card accepted

Open: Year round except New Year

Description: Visit Hele Valley and experience the peace and tranquillity of this natural holiday park offering luxury cottages, superb lodges, stylish caravans and camping.

Facilities:

To Beach: 0.49 miles

ILFRACOMBE – TUNNELS BEACHES

Dilkhusa Grand Hotel

♦♦♦Guest Accommodation

Wilder Road, Ilfracombe, Devon, EX34 9AH

T: +44 (0) 1942 824824
E: reservations@washearings.com
W: washearings.com

Bedrooms: 98 • £56.00-£97.00 per double room per night, breakfast included • Debit/credit card; cheques/cash accepted

Open: Seasonal opening – call for details

Description: On the sea front overlooking Runnymede Gardens, the hotel is only a few minutes' walk from the beaches and harbour. Entertainment every night.

Facilities:

To Beach: 0.5 miles

ILFRACOMBE – TUNNELS BEACHES

St Brannocks House Hotel

★★Hotel

61 St Brannocks Road, Ilfracombe, Devon, EX34 8EQ

T: +44 (0) 1271 863873
E: stbrannocks@aol.com
W: stbrannockshotel.co.uk

Bedrooms: 6 • £64.00 per double room per night, breakfast included • Debit/credit card; cheques/cash accepted

Open: Seasonal opening – call for details

Description: Dog-friendly hotel in level position within walking distance of town and seafront. Licensed premises. Car parking for all.

Facilities:

To Beach: 0.81 miles

ILFRACOMBE – TUNNELS BEACHES

The Darnley Hotel ★★Hotel

3 Belmont Road, Ilfracombe, Devon, EX34 8DR

T:	+44 (0) 1271 863955
E:	darnleyhotel@yahoo.co.uk
W:	darnleyhotel.co.uk
Bedrooms:	10 • £48.00-£80.00 per double room per night, breakfast included • Debit/credit card; cheques/cash accepted
Open:	Year round
Description:	An elegant, Victorian, family-run hotel with a licensed bar, plus restaurant serving home-cooked meals. All rooms either en suite or private facilities with colour TV, clock, radio and beverage-making facilities. Ample private parking.
Facilities:	
To Beach:	0.79 miles

ILFRACOMBE – TUNNELS BEACHES

The Torrs Hotel ★Hotel

Torrs Park, Ilfracombe, Devon, EX34 8AY

T:	+44 (0) 1271 862334
E:	torrshotel@aol.com
W:	thetorrshotel.co.uk
Bedrooms:	11 • £50.00-£60.00 per double room per night, breakfast included • Debit/credit card accepted
Open:	Year round except New Year
Description:	This elegant, Victorian mansion has been continually upgraded over recent years to provide all the amenities required by today's discerning guest.
Facilities:	P
To Beach:	0.79 miles

ILFRACOMBE – TUNNELS BEACHES

Varley House ★★★★Guest Accommodation

Chambercombe Park, Ilfracombe, Devon, EX34 9QW

T:	+44 (0) 1271 863927
E:	info@varleyhouse.co.uk
W:	varleyhouse.co.uk
Bedrooms:	8 • £56.00-£68.00 per double room per night, breakfast included • Debit/credit card; cheques/cash accepted
Open:	Year round
Description:	Friendly, family-run house with comfortable, well-furnished rooms. Evening meal is available. It has a bar, garden and its own parking in a quiet location overlooking the harbour.
Facilities:	P
To Beach:	0.41 miles

ILFRACOMBE – TUNNELS BEACHES

Widmouth Farm Cottages ★★★B&B

Watermouth, Ilfracombe, Devon, EX34 9RX

T:	+44 (0) 1271 863743
E:	holiday@widmouthfarmcottages.co.uk
W:	widmouthfarmcottages.co.uk
Bedrooms:	4 • £55.00 per double room per night, breakfast included
Open:	Seasonal opening – call for details
Description:	Spectacular views, private beach and wonderful coastal walks. Exclusive use of comfortable cottage and breakfast in magnificent farmhouse kitchen overlooking sea!
Facilities:	
To Beach:	0.66 miles

MAIDENCOMBE – WATCOMBE BEACH

English House Hotel and Restaurant

♦♦♦♦Guest Accommodation

Teignmouth Road, Maidencombe, Torquay, Devon, TQ1 4SY

T:	+44 (0) 1803 328760
E:	englishhouse@maidencombedevon.freeserve.co.uk
W:	english-house.co.uk
Bedrooms:	3 • £70.00-£90.00 per double room per night, breakfast included • Debit/credit card; cheques/cash accepted
Open:	Year round except Christmas and New Year
Description:	Relaxing restaurant and rooms with modern style throughout. The chef is London-trained chef. Winner of 2004 Best Dining Out, an English Riviera award.
Facilities:	
To Beach:	0.5 miles

MALBOROUGH – HOPE COVE

Bolberry House Farm

★★★Holiday, Touring & Caravan Park

Bolberry, Malborough, Kingsbridge, Devon, TQ7 3DY

T:	+44 (0) 1548 561251
E:	bolberry.house@virgin.net
W:	bolberryparks.co.uk
Pitches:	104 • £7.50-£10.50 per caravan per night
Open:	Seasonal opening – call for details
Description:	Located in a beautiful coastal area, this friendly family park is peaceful and level with good facilities. Children's play area. Good access to coastal footpaths and sandy beaches nearby. A small shop is open in high season.
Facilities:	
To Beach:	1.04 miles

MALBOROUGH – SALCOMBE SOUTH

Higher Rew Touring Caravan & Camping Park

★★★★Camping & Touring Park

Higher Rew, Malborough, Kingsbridge, Devon, TQ7 3DW

T: +44 (0) 1548 842681
E: enquiries@higherrew.co.uk
W: higherrew.co.uk

Pitches: 270 • £7.00-£12.00 per caravan per night

Open: Seasonal opening – call for details

Description: Five-acre site that is gently sloping, but terraced, providing level pitches in Area of Outstanding Natural Beauty just a mile from the beach.

Facilities:

To Beach: 0.99 miles

MARLDON – HOLLACOMBE BEACH

Widdicombe Farm Touring Park

★★★★Holiday, Touring & Caravan Park

Marldon, Paignton, Devon, TQ3 1ST

T: +44 (0) 1803 558325
E: info@widdicombefarm.co.uk
W: Torquaytouring.co.uk

Pitches: 233 • £7.00-£17.50 per caravan per night • Debit/credit card; cheques/cash accepted

Open: Seasonal opening – call for details

Description: The nearest touring and caravan park to Torquay's town and beaches. This select, family-run park is easy to find. No narrow country lanes. Luxurious facilities. The park also has three holiday six-berth caravans to let.

Facilities:

To Beach: 1.88 miles

MORTEHOE – WOOLACOMBE SANDS

North Morte Farm Caravan and Camping Park

★★★★Holiday, Touring & Caravan Park

North Morte Road, Mortehoe, Woolacombe, Devon, EX34 7EG

T: +44 (0) 1271 870381
E: info@northmortefarm.co.uk
W: northmortefarm.co.uk

Pitches: 224 • £10.00-£17.00 per caravan per night • Debit/credit card accepted

Open: Seasonal opening – call for details

Description: Nearest caravan park to sea in the area. Secluded and in beautiful coastal country, six miles from Ilfracombe. Four-, six- and eight-berth vans. Shop, laundry room, parking, phone and children's play area all on site.

Facilities:

To Beach: 1.85 miles

NORTHAM – WESTWARD HO!

Riversford Hotel ★★Hotel

Limers Lane, Northam, Bideford, Devon, EX39 2RG

T: +44 (0) 1237 474239
E: riversford@aol.com
W: riversford.co.uk

Bedrooms: 15 • £75.00-£110.00 per double room per night, breakfast included • Debit/credit card; cheques/cash accepted

Open: Year round

Description: Riversford is a peacefully located hotel with stunning views over the River Torridge. Locally produced foods and close to lots of amenities.

Facilities:

To Beach: 1.38 miles

PAIGNTON – BREAKWATER BEACH

Benbows Hotel ★★★Guest Accommodation

1 Alta Vista Road, Roundham, Paignton, Devon, TQ4 6DB

T: +44 (0) 1803 558128
E: benbowshotel@btinternet.com
W: benbowshotel.co.uk

Bedrooms: 10 • £36.00-£46.00 per double room per night, breakfast included • Debit/credit card; cheques/cash accepted

Open: Year round

Description: Attractive, licensed, family-run hotel, near tranquil gardens in Roundham Point, between Paignton and Goodrington beaches some 120 yards from harbour.

Facilities: P

To Beach: 0.29 miles

PAIGNTON – BREAKWATER BEACH

Queens Hotel ★★Hotel

Queens Road, Paignton, Devon, TQ4 6AT

T: +44 (0) 1803 551048
E: info@queensPaignton.com
W: queensPaignton.com

Bedrooms: 76 • £54.00-£86.00 per double room per night, breakfast included • Debit/credit card accepted

Open: Year round

Description: At the Queen's Hotel where you will enjoy the 76 en suite bedrooms, the indoor, heated pool, games room, entertainment with dance floor, and private car park.

Facilities:

To Beach: 0.18 miles

PAIGNTON – BREAKWATER BEACH

Seaways Hotel ♦♦♦♦Guest Accommodation

30 Sands Road, Paignton, Devon, TQ4 6EJ

T: +44 (0) 1803 551093
E: seawayshotel@aol.com
W: seawayshotel.com

Bedrooms: 11 • £44.00-£56.00 per double room per night, breakfast included • Debit/credit card; cheques/cash accepted

Open: Year round

Description: Small, luxury hotel on Paignton seafront with spectacular views over Torbay. There is a residents' bar and lounge. All bedrooms have en suite facilities.

Facilities:

To Beach: 0.09 miles

PAIGNTON – BREAKWATER BEACH

Two Beaches Hotel ★★★★Guest Accommodation

27 St Andrews Road, Paignton, Devon, TQ4 6HA

T: +44 (0) 1803 522164
E: stay@twobeaches.co.uk
W: twobeaches.co.uk

Bedrooms: 7 • £45.00-£52.00 per double room per night, breakfast included • Cheques/cash accepted

Open: Year round except Christmas and New Year

Description: High quality, non-smoking, family-run hotel in a quiet area close to the harbour and amenities. Warm, relaxed atmosphere and good, home-cooked food.

Facilities: P

To Beach: 0.24 miles

PAIGNTON – BREAKWATER BEACH

Wynncroft Hotel ★★★Guest Accommodation

Elmsleigh Park, Paignton, Devon, TQ4 5AT

T: +44 (0) 1803 525728
E: wynncroft@FSBDial.co.uk
W: wynncroft.co.uk

Bedrooms: 11 • £50.00-£64.00 per double room per night, breakfast included • Debit/credit card accepted

Open: Year round except New Year

Description: A family-run, licensed, Victorian hotel, in a quiet road five minutes from sea and shops, excellent food and service for normal and special dietary needs.

Facilities: P

To Beach: 0.39 miles

PAIGNTON – BROADSANDS

Culverden Guesthouse ★★★Guest Accommodation

4 Colin Road, Paignton, Devon, TQ3 2NR

T:	+44 (0) 1803 559786
E:	info@culverdenhotel.co.uk
W:	culverdenhotel.co.uk
Bedrooms:	8 • £36.00-£52.00 per double room per night, breakfast included • Debit/credit card accepted
Open:	Year round
Description:	Small, family-run, non-smoking guesthouse with en suite and family rooms plus parking. It's a 10-minute, level walk from town, bus and train.
Facilities:	
To Beach:	0.13 miles

PAIGNTON – GOODRINGTON SOUTH

Cherra Hotel ♦♦♦Guest Accommodation

15 Roundham Road, Paignton, Devon, TQ4 6DN

T:	+44 (0) 1803 550723
E:	info@cherra-hotel.co.uk
W:	cherra-hotel.co.uk
Bedrooms:	12 • £50.00-£60.00 per double room per night, breakfast included • Debit/credit card accepted
Open:	Year round except Christmas and New Year
Description:	Friendly, family-run, licensed hotel. Owners aim to pull out all the stops to meet visitors' needs and make their holiday complete.
Facilities:	
To Beach:	0.27 miles

PAIGNTON – GOODRINGTON SOUTH

Marine Park Holiday Centre

★★★★Holiday & Touring Park

Grange Road, Paignton, Devon, TQ4 7JR

T:	+44 (0) 1803 843887
E:	info@beverley-holidays.co.uk
W:	beverley-holidays.co.uk
Pitches:	103 • £12.00-£20.50 per caravan per night • Debit/credit card; cheques/cash accepted
Open:	Seasonal opening – call for details
Description:	Nestling on the hillside, in a peaceful surrounding with superb views of Torbay, Marine Park offers touring holiday caravan homes.
Facilities:	
To Beach:	0.5 miles

PAIGNTON – GOODRINGTON SOUTH

The Old School House B&B ★★★★★B&B

Blagdon Road, Collaton St Mary, Paignton, Devon, TQ3 3YA

T: +44 (0) 1803 523011
E: abdy13@tiscali.co.uk
W: oldschoolhousedevon.co.uk

Bedrooms: 2 • £70.00 per double room per night, breakfast included

Open: Year round except Christmas and New Year

Description: The Old School House offers two very comfortable rooms, a hearty breakfast and a warm welcome. Single occupancy available on request.

Facilities:

To Beach: 1.84 miles

PAIGNTON – PAIGNTON BEACH

Bella Vista Guesthouse ★★★Guest Accommodation

Berry Square, Paignton, Devon, TQ4 6AZ

T: +44 (0) 1803 558122
E: bellavista@berrysquare.fsbusiness.co.uk
W: english-riviera.co.uk/accommodation/guest-houses/bella-vista/index.htm

Bedrooms: 8 • £38.00-£50.00 per double room per night, breakfast included • Debit/credit card; cheques/cash accepted

Open: Seasonal opening – call for details

Description: Situated in a garden square adjacent to seafront and town. Separate tables and choice of menu. Also there are colour TVs and tea-makers in all rooms.

Facilities: P

To Beach: 0.06 miles

PAIGNTON – PAIGNTON BEACH

Beresford Hotel ♦♦♦♦Guest Accommodation

5 Adelphi Road, Paignton, Devon, TQ4 6AW SILVER AWARD

T: +44 (0) 1803 551560
E: info@beresfordhotel.co.uk
W: beresfordhotel.co.uk

Bedrooms: 8 • £42.00-£56.00 per double room per night, breakfast included • Debit/credit card accepted

Open: Year round

Description: Small, friendly hotel close to beach, town centre, rail and coach stations. A quality, comfortable and relaxed venue which is superbly situated in a quiet location.

Facilities:

To Beach: 0.15 miles

PAIGNTON – PAIGNTON BEACH

Blue Waters Guesthouse ★★★★Guest Accommodation

4 Leighon Road, Paignton, Devon, TQ3 2BQ

T:	+44 (0) 1803 557749
E:	bluewatershotel@aol.com
W:	bluewatershotel.co.uk
Bedrooms:	6 • £35.00-£50.00 per double room per night, breakfast included • Debit/credit card accepted
Open:	Year round except Christmas and New Year
Description:	Described by the owners as the "quiet alternative" – a warm, friendly greeting awaits you at this comfortable guesthouse. Close to seafront and holiday attractions.
Facilities:	
To Beach:	0.2 miles

PAIGNTON – PAIGNTON BEACH

Carrington Guesthouse ★★★Guesthouse

10 Beach Road, Paignton, Devon, TQ4 6AY

T:	+44 (0) 1803 558785
E:	info@carringtonguesthouse.co.uk
W:	carringtonguesthouse.co.uk
Bedrooms:	10 • £32.00-£48.00 per double room per night, breakfast included • Debit/credit card accepted
Open:	Seasonal opening – call for details
Description:	The Carrington is a family-run B&B which can be found 100 yards from Paignton seafront and close to all amenities.
Facilities:	
To Beach:	0.1 miles

PAIGNTON – PAIGNTON BEACH

Garfield Lodge ★★★★Guest Accommodation

30 Garfield Road, Paignton, Devon, TQ4 6AX

T:	+44 (0) 1803 557764
E:	garfieldlodge1@aol.com
W:	garfieldlodge.co.uk
Bedrooms:	22 • £40.00-£50.00 per double room per night, breakfast included • Debit/credit card accepted
Open:	Seasonal opening – call for details
Description:	Family-run guesthouse, comfortable and well decorated, with a friendly atmosphere that lies close to town centre, railway/coach stations and beach.
Facilities:	
To Beach:	0.1 miles

PAIGNTON – PAIGNTON BEACH

Norbreck ★★★Guesthouse

New Street, Paignton, Devon, TQ3 3HL

T:	+44 (0) 1803 558033
E:	norbreckguesthouse@hotmail.com
W:	norbreck.com
Bedrooms:	7 • £32.00-£36.00 per twin room per night, breakfast included • Debit/credit card accepted
Open:	Year round
Description:	Licensed, family-run, friendly guesthouse, providing good, home-cooked food. On level, close to bus, rail and all amenities.
Facilities:	
To Beach:	0.44 miles

PAIGNTON – PAIGNTON BEACH

Rockview Guesthouse ♦♦♦Guest Accommodation

13 Queens Road, Paignton, Devon, TQ4 6AT

T:	+44 (0) 1803 556702
E:	rockview@blueyonder.co.uk
W:	rockview.co.uk
Bedrooms:	7 • £34.00-£42.00 per double room per night, breakfast included • Debit/credit card accepted
Open:	Year round except Christmas and New Year
Description:	Ideally situated for easy, level walk to shops, harbour and seafront. The owners bid you welcome.
Facilities:	
To Beach:	0.18 miles

PAIGNTON – PAIGNTON BEACH

The Palace Hotel ★★★Hotel

Esplanade Road, Paignton, Devon, TQ4 6BJ

T:	+44 (0) 1803 555121
E:	info@palacePaignton.com
W:	palacePaignton.com
Bedrooms:	56 • £80.00-£100.00 per double room per night, breakfast included • Debit/credit card accepted
Open:	Year round
Description:	Standing in prime, seafront location with acres of semi-tropical gardens plus extensive views across Torbay.
Facilities:	
To Beach:	0.19 miles

PAIGNTON – PAIGNTON BEACH

Waverley Guesthouse ♦♦♦Guest Accommodation

9 Warefield Road, Paignton, Devon, TQ3 2BH

T:	+44 (0) 1803 551027
E:	janie@waverleygh.co.uk
W:	waverleygh.co.uk
Bedrooms:	7 • £34.00-£50.00 per double room per night, breakfast included • Debit/credit card accepted
Open:	Year round except Christmas
Description:	The resident hosts bid you a warm welcome to their friendly and relaxed, family-run guesthouse.
Facilities:	
To Beach:	0.26 miles

SALCOMBE – SALCOMBE SOUTH SANDS

Salcombe YHA ★★★Hostel

Overbecks, Sharpitor, Salcombe, Devon, TQ8 8LW

T:	+44 (0) 1548 842856
E:	salcombe@yha.org.uk
W:	yha.org.uk
Dormitories:	11 • £10.00-£13.50 per person per night, room only • Debit/credit card; cheques/cash accepted
Open:	Seasonal opening – call for details
Description:	Six acres of semi-tropical gardens surround the elegant, Edwardian house in this National Trust property.
Facilities:	
To Beach:	0.23 miles

SALCOMBE – SALCOMBE SOUTH SANDS

Tides Reach Hotel ★★★Hotel

GOLD AWARD

Cliff Road, Salcombe, Devon, TQ8 8LJ

T:	+44 (0) 1548 843466
E:	enquire@tidesreach.com
W:	tidesreach.com
Bedrooms:	35 • £110.00-£250.00 per double room per night, breakfast included • Debit/credit card; cheques/cash accepted
Open:	Seasonal opening – call for details
Description:	Elegant and well-appointed hotel in an unrivalled position of natural beauty on edge of a secluded, tree-fringed, sandy cove.
Facilities:	
To Beach:	0.14 miles

SOUTH MILTON – THURLESTONE BEACH

Shute Farm

★★★Guest Accommodation

South Milton, Kingsbridge, Devon, TQ7 3JL

T: +44 (0) 1548 560680
E: luscombe@shutefarm.fsnet.co.uk
W: shutefarm.co.uk

Bedrooms: 3 • £44.00-£48.00 per double room per night, breakfast included

Open: Year round

Description: Lovely, old farmhouse with plenty of character and oak-beamed lounge. Situated in a quiet position only a little more than 1.5 miles from Thurlestone Sands.

Facilities:

To Beach: 1.64 miles

STARCROSS – DAWLISH WARREN BEACH

Cofton Country Holidays

★★★Holiday, Touring & Camping Park

Cofton, Starcross, Exeter, Devon, EX6 8RP

ROSE AWARD

T: +44 (0) 1626 890111
E: info@coftonholidays.co.uk
W: coftonholidays.co.uk

Pitches: 1416 • £12.00-£19.50 per caravan per night • Debit/credit card; cheques/cash accepted

Open: Year round except Christmas and New Year

Description: Situated in open countryside near sandy beach on A379, three miles the Exeter side of Dawlish. Ideal touring centre. Family area in bar serving food.

Facilities: P

To Beach: 1.25 miles

STOKE FLEMING – BLACKPOOL SANDS

Stoke Lodge Hotel

★★★Hotel

Cinders Lane, Stoke Fleming, Dartmouth, Devon, TQ6 0RA

T: +44 (0) 1803 770523
E: mail@stokelodge.co.uk
W: stokelodge.co.uk

Bedrooms: 25 • £87.00-£112.00 per double room per night, breakfast included • Debit/credit card; cheques/cash accepted

Open: Year round

Description: Country house hotel near the sea enjoying lovely views. Indoor and outdoor pools. Leisure facilities include a tennis court.

Facilities:

To Beach: 0.62 miles

STRETE – BLACKPOOL SANDS

Skerries B&B

★★★★Guest Accommodation
Strete, Dartmouth, Devon, TQ6 0RH
SILVER AWARD

T: +44 (0) 1803 770775
E: jam.skerries@rya-online.net
W: skerriesbandb.co.uk

Bedrooms: 3 • £58.00-£70.00 per double room per night, breakfast included • Cheques/cash accepted

Open: Year round except Christmas

Description: A modern house with stunning views over Start Bay. Relaxed, friendly atmosphere in quality surroundings. Between Blackpool Sands and Slapton Ley.

Facilities:

To Beach: 0.92 miles

STRETE – BLACKPOOL SANDS

Strete Barton Farmhouse

★★★★Guest Accommodation
Totnes Road, Strete, Dartmouth, Devon, TQ6 0RN
SILVER AWARD

T: +44 (0) 1803 770364
E: david@stretebarton.co.uk
W: stretebarton.co.uk

Bedrooms: 6 • £65.00-£85.00 per double room per night, breakfast included • Debit/credit card; cheques/cash accepted

Open: Year round except Christmas

Description: 16thC farmhouse with stunning sea views. Six exquisitely furnished bedrooms either en suite or private facilities. English or continental breakfast.

Facilities: P

To Beach: 1.05 miles

TEIGNMOUTH

The Moorings

★★★★★Guest Accommodation
33 Teignmouth Road, Teignmouth, Devon, TQ14 8UR

T: +44 (0) 1626 770400
E: mickywaters@aol.com
W: visitwestcountry.com/themoorings

Bedrooms: 1 • £60.00-£65.00 per double room per night, breakfast included

Open: Year round

Description: Spectacular, uninterrupted 180 degree sea views of Babbacombe Bay and Lyme Bay with all their water activities. Double, luxurious room has en suite, colour TV, tea-/coffee-making facilities, wine fridge and own conservatory.

Facilities: P TV

To Beach: 1.11 miles

TEIGNMOUTH

Thomas Luny House ★★★★★Guest Accommodation

Teign Street, Teignmouth, Devon, TQ14 8EG GOLD AWARD

T: +44 (0) 1626 772976
E: alisonandjohn@thomas-luny-house.co.uk
W: thomas-luny-house.co.uk

Bedrooms: 4 • £76.00-£92.00 per double room per night, breakfast included • Debit/credit card; cheques/cash accepted

Open: Year round

Description: Georgian, licensed B&B in level position in old quarter of town. Walled garden for guests. Ample car parking.

Facilities:

To Beach: 0.26 miles

TEIGNMOUTH

Thornhill Hotel ★★★★Guest Accommodation

Mere Lane, Teignmouth, Devon, TQ14 8TA

T: +44 (0) 1626 773460
E: information@thornhillhotelteignmouth.co.uk
W: thornhillhotelteignmouth.co.uk

Bedrooms: 9 • £50.00-£55.00 per double room per night, breakfast included

Open: Year round except Christmas and New Year

Description: Friendly, family-run seafront hotel. Excellent home cooking. Level location. Ground floor bedroom and public rooms.

Facilities:

To Beach: 0.12 miles

THURLESTONE

Thurlestone Hotel ★★★★Hotel

Thurlestone, Kingsbridge, Devon, TQ7 3NN GOLD AWARD

T: +44 (0) 1548 560382
E: enquiries@thurlestone.co.uk
W: thurlestone.co.uk

Bedrooms: 64 • £100.00-£232.00 per double room per night, breakfast included • Debit/credit card; cheques/cash accepted

Open: Year round

Description: A peaceful setting in village of thatched cottages, Thurlestone Hotel offers international cuisine and outstanding indoor and outdoor sporting amenities, including a golf course.

Facilities:

To Beach: 0.5 miles

TORQUAY – ANSTEY'S COVE

Palace Hotel

★★★★Hotel
SILVER AWARD

Babbacombe Road, Torquay, Devon, TQ1 3TG

T:	+44 (0) 1803 200200
E:	info@palaceTorquay.co.uk
W:	palaceTorquay.co.uk
Bedrooms:	141 • £130.00-£228.00 per double room per night, breakfast included • Debit/credit card; cheques/cash accepted
Open:	Year round
Description:	Beautifully set in 25 acres leading to Anstey's Cove. Exceptionally high standard of service, excellent cuisine and unrivalled leisure facilities.
Facilities:	[symbols]
To Beach:	0.19 miles

TORQUAY – BABBACOMBE BEACH

Regency Hotel

★★Hotel

33-35 Babbacombe Downs Road, Torquay, Devon, TQ1 3LN

T:	+44 (0) 1803 323509
E:	theregency@hotmail.com
W:	regencyTorquay.co.uk
Bedrooms:	22 • £50.00-£60.00 per double room per night, breakfast included • Debit/credit card accepted
Open:	Seasonal opening – call for details
Description:	The hotel is on the seafront overlooking Lynne Bay, on the beautiful Babbacombe Downs, three-quarters of the rooms have sea views.
Facilities:	[symbols]
To Beach:	0.18 miles

TORQUAY – CORBYN HEAD (TORRE ABBEY)

Abbeyfield Hotel

♦♦♦♦Guest Accommodation

Bridge Road, Torquay, Devon, TQ2 5AX

T:	+44 (0) 1803 294268
E:	abbeyfieldhotel@amserve.com
W:	abbeyfield-hotel.co.uk
Bedrooms:	6 • £40.00-£64.00 per double room per night, breakfast included • Debit/credit card; cheques/cash accepted
Open:	Year round except Christmas
Description:	A comfortable, detached, period hotel set in south-facing gardens and centrally situated for visiting Torquay and the Riviera. All bedrooms have en suite facilities.
Facilities:	P[symbols]
To Beach:	0.34 miles

TORQUAY – CORBYN HEAD (TORRE ABBEY)

Brampton Court Hotel ♦♦♦Guest Accommodation

St Lukes Road South, Torquay, Devon, TQ2 5NZ

T: +44 (0) 1803 294237
E: stay@bramptoncourt.co.uk
W: bramptoncourt.co.uk

Bedrooms: 20 • £50.00-£75.00 per double room per night, breakfast included • Debit/credit card accepted

Open: Year round

Description: All rooms en suite. Family-run and friendly atmosphere. Peaceful location with views over Torbay. Convenient for town, seafront and Riviera Centre.

Facilities:

To Beach: 0.29 miles

TORQUAY – CORBYN HEAD (TORRE ABBEY)

Briarfields Hotel ★★Guest Accommodation

84/86 Avenue Road, Torquay, Devon, TQ2 5LF

T: +44 (0) 1803 297844
E: briarfieldshotel@aol.com
W: rfields.co.uk

Bedrooms: 9 • £35.00-£45.00 per double room per night, breakfast included • Debit/credit card accepted

Open: Year round except Christmas and New Year

Description: Friendly accommodation offering bed and hearty breakfast. Short, flat walk to seafront. Private car park. Pet-friendly.

Facilities: P

To Beach: 0.5 miles

TORQUAY – CORBYN HEAD (TORRE ABBEY)

Bute Court Hotel ★★Hotel

Belgrave Road, Torquay, Devon, TQ2 5HQ

T: +44 (0) 1803 213055
E: stay@butecourthotel.co.uk
W: butecourthotel.co.uk

Bedrooms: 44 • £52.00-£94.00 per double room per night, breakfast included • Debit/credit card; cheques/cash accepted

Open: Year round

Description: Family-run hotel overlooking Torbay and adjoining Riviera Centre. Large lounges and bar. Five-course choice menu.

Facilities:

To Beach: 0.14 miles

TORQUAY – CORBYN HEAD (TORRE ABBEY)

Carlton Hotel

★★★Hotel

Falkland Road, Torquay, Devon, TQ2 5JJ

T:	+44 (0) 1803 400300
E:	jbrowne@tlh.co.uk
W:	tlh.co.uk
Bedrooms:	55 • £80.00-£126.00 per double room per night, breakfast included • Debit/credit card; cheques/cash accepted
Open:	Year round
Description:	The Carlton has 55 bedrooms and 10 self-catering apartments, with a friendly, intimate atmosphere. Situated on the level and close to the seafront, it offers excellent cuisine.
Facilities:	[icons]
To Beach:	0.28 miles

TORQUAY – CORBYN HEAD (TORRE ABBEY)

Carlton Court Hotel

★★Hotel
SILVER AWARD

18 Cleveland Road, Torquay, Devon, TQ2 5BE

T:	+44 (0) 1803 297318
E:	stay@carlton-court.co.uk
W:	carlton-court.co.uk
Bedrooms:	8 • £58.00-£148.00 per double room per night, breakfast included • Debit/credit card accepted
Open:	Year round
Description:	Lovely, detached, Victorian villa, set in a peaceful part of Torquay, yet only a short walk from the beach, theatre and shops.
Facilities:	[icons]
To Beach:	0.5 miles

TORQUAY – CORBYN HEAD (TORRE ABBEY)

Cloudlands

★★★★Guest Accommodation

St Agnes Lane, Torquay, Devon, TQ2 6QD

T:	+44 (0) 1803 606550
E:	cloudlands.Torquay@yahoo.co.uk
W:	cloudlands.co.uk
Bedrooms:	10 • £44.00-£50.00 per double room per night, breakfast included • Debit/credit card accepted
Open:	Year round
Description:	Cloudlands offers visitors the ambience of a private home, yet at the same time all the amenities of a small hotel. It is in a peaceful position within a conservation area just a short stroll from the seafront.
Facilities:	[icons]
To Beach:	0.34 miles

TORQUAY – CORBYN HEAD (TORRE ABBEY)

Colindale Hotel ★★★★Guest Accommodation

20 Rathmore Road, Torquay, Devon, TQ2 6NY

T:	+44 (0) 1803 293947
E:	bronte@eurobell.co.uk
W:	colindalehotel.co.uk
Bedrooms:	8 • £32.50-£35.00 per double room per night, breakfast included • Debit/credit card; cheques/cash accepted
Open:	Year round except Christmas and New Year
Description:	A Victorian house of great charm, on the edge of Torre Abbey Gardens, with spacious, well-furnished rooms. Short, level walk from railway station and seafront.
Facilities:	
To Beach:	0.27 miles

TORQUAY – CORBYN HEAD (TORRE ABBEY)

Crowndale Hotel ★★★★Guest Accommodation

18 Bridge Road, Torquay, Devon, TR12 7HB

T:	+44 (0) 1803 293068
E:	info@crowndalehotel.co.uk
W:	crowndalehotel.co.uk
Bedrooms:	7 • £44.00-£52.00 per double room per night, breakfast included • Debit/credit card accepted
Open:	Year round
Description:	At the non-smoking Crowndale, the owners offer their guests good food, comfortable accommodation and, above all, a friendly welcome.
Facilities:	P
To Beach:	0.42 miles

TORQUAY – CORBYN HEAD (TORRE ABBEY)

Crimdon Dene Hotel ♦♦♦Guest Accommodation

Falkland Road, Torquay, Devon, TQ2 5JP

T:	+44 (0) 1803 294651
E:	marjohn@crimdondenehotel.co.uk
W:	crimdondenehotel.co.uk
Bedrooms:	10 • £38.00-£54.00 per double room per night, breakfast included • Debit/credit card accepted
Open:	Year round
Description:	Friendly, licensed, non-smoking establishment. Walking distance to rail station, beach and town centre. Families welcome, has ground floor rooms and own car park.
Facilities:	
To Beach:	0.32 miles

TORQUAY – CORBYN HEAD (TORRE ABBEY)

Ferndale Hotel ♦♦♦♦Guest Accommodation

22 St Marychurch Road, Torquay, Devon, TQ1 3HY

T:	+44 (0) 1803 295311
E:	jan.ferndale@btinternet.com
W:	ferndalehotel-Torquay.co.uk
Bedrooms:	22 • £44.00-£54.00 per double room per night, breakfast included
Open:	Year round except Christmas and New Year
Description:	All rooms are en suite. Short walk to the sea and about 300 yards from the town centre. Evening meals available.
Facilities:	[icons]
To Beach:	0.49 miles

TORQUAY – CORBYN HEAD (TORRE ABBEY)

Glenross Hotel ♦♦♦♦Guest Accommodation

25 Avenue Road, Torquay, Devon, TQ2 5LB SILVER AWARD

T:	+44 (0) 1803 297517
E:	holiday@glenross-hotel.co.uk
W:	glenross-hotel.co.uk
Bedrooms:	12 • £46.00-£54.00 per double room per night, breakfast included • Debit/credit card accepted
Open:	Seasonal opening – call for details
Description:	Family-owned, centrally located, hotel enjoying pleasant accommodation, food and company.
Facilities:	[icons]
To Beach:	0.42 miles

TORQUAY – CORBYN HEAD (TORRE ABBEY)

Grosvenor House Hotel ★★★★Guest Accommodation

Falkland Road, Torquay, Devon, TQ2 5JP

T:	+44 (0) 1803 294110
E:	etc@grosvenorhousehotel.co.uk
W:	grosvenorhousehotel.co.uk
Bedrooms:	10 • £42.00 per double room per night, breakfast included • Debit/credit card; cheques/cash accepted
Open:	Seasonal opening – call for details
Description:	Comfortable, licensed hotel in quiet central area, run by Christian family. Excellent home-cooked food with choice of menu.
Facilities:	[icons]
To Beach:	0.3 miles

TORQUAY – CORBYN HEAD (TORRE ABBEY)

Kingston House ♦♦♦♦♦Guest Accommodation

75 Avenue Road, Torquay, Devon, TQ2 5LL SILVER AWARD

T: +44 (0) 1803 212760
E: butto@kingstonhousehotel.co.uk
W: stonhousehotel.co.uk

Bedrooms: 5 • £50.00-£69.00 per double room per night, breakfast included • Debit/credit card; cheques/cash accepted

Open: Seasonal opening – call for details

Description: Victorian elegance with modern amenities. Beautifully appointed en suite rooms. Level walk to seafront, harbour and town. Private parking.

Facilities:

To Beach: 0.62 miles

TORQUAY – CORBYN HEAD (TORRE ABBEY)

Lindum Hotel ♦♦♦♦Guest Accommodation

105 Abbey Road, Torquay, Devon, TQ2 5NP

T: +44 (0) 1803 292795
E: enquiries@lindum-hotel.co.uk
W: lindum-hotel.co.uk

Bedrooms: 17 • £50.00-£66.00 per double room per night, breakfast included • Debit/credit card; cheques/cash accepted

Open: Year round except Christmas and New Year

Description: Centrally located with roomy en suite bedrooms, all designated non-smoking, licensed bar, delightful sun terrace and secure on-site parking. Ideal for independent travellers.

Facilities:

To Beach: 0.35 miles

TORQUAY – CORBYN HEAD (TORRE ABBEY)

Livermead House Hotel ★★★Hotel

Torbay Road, Torquay, Devon, TQ2 6QJ

T: +44 (0) 1803 294361
E: info@livermead.com
W: livermead.com

Bedrooms: 67 • £92.00-£168.00 per double room per night, breakfast included • Debit/credit card; cheques/cash accepted

Open: Year round

Description: Close to the town centre on Torbay Road. Waterfront location, built in 1820. One-time home of author Charles Kingsley.

Facilities:

To Beach: 0.5 miles

TORQUAY – CORBYN HEAD (TORRE ABBEY)

Rawlyn House Hotel ★★Hotel

Rawlyn Road, Chelston, Torquay, Devon, TQ2 6PL

T:	+44 (0) 1803 605208
E:	shirley@rawlynhousehotel.co.uk
W:	rawlynhousehotel.co.uk
Bedrooms:	12 • £86.00-£108.00 per double room per night, breakfast included • Debit/credit card; cheques/cash accepted
Open:	Seasonal opening – call for details
Description:	A charming Victorian country house standing in quiet secluded grounds, where comfort and quality matter.
Facilities:	
To Beach:	0.62 miles

TORQUAY – CORBYN HEAD (TORRE ABBEY)

Red House Hotel ★★Hotel

Rousdown Road, Torquay, Devon, TQ2 6PB

T:	+44 (0) 1803 607811
E:	stay@redhouse-hotel.co.uk
W:	redhouse-hotel.co.uk
Bedrooms:	10 • £48.00-£76.00 per double room per night, breakfast included • Debit/credit card accepted
Open:	Year round
Description:	Small, friendly hotel offering indoor/outdoor pools, spa, sauna, gym and beauty salon. Adjoining self-catering or serviced apartments. Convenient for seafront and other amenities.
Facilities:	P
To Beach:	0.36 miles

TORQUAY – CORBYN HEAD (TORRE ABBEY)

The Haven Hotel ♦♦♦♦Guest Accommodation

11 Scarborough Road, Torquay, Devon, TQ2 5UJ

T:	+44 (0) 1803 293390
E:	enquiries@havenhotel.biz
W:	havenhotel.biz
Bedrooms:	6 • £30.00-£60.00 per double room per night, breakfast included • Debit/credit card; cheques/cash accepted
Open:	Year round
Description:	Delightful, small, family-run hotel. Relaxed and comfortable. Good food. Off Belgrave Road, close to beach, shops and Riviera centre.
Facilities:	P
To Beach:	0.31 miles

TORQUAY – CORBYN HEAD (TORRE ABBEY)

The Southbank Hotel ♦♦♦♦Guest Accommodation

15-17 Belgrave Road, Torquay, Devon, TQ2 5HU

T:	+44 (0) 1803 296701
E:	stay@southbankhotel.co.uk
W:	southbankhotel.co.uk
Bedrooms:	16 • £44.00-£51.00 per double room per night, breakfast included • Debit/credit card accepted
Open:	Year round except Christmas
Description:	Family-run, licensed hotel open all year round. Close to bay and convention/leisure centre in central location. Evening meals available.
Facilities:	
To Beach:	0.28 miles

TORQUAY – CORBYN HEAD (TORRE ABBEY)

Torbay Hotel ♦♦♦♦Guest Accommodation

Torbay Road, Torquay, Devon, TQ2 5EY

T:	+44 (0) 1942 824824
E:	b.pitman@washearings.com
W:	washearings.com
Bedrooms:	112 • £50.00-£88.00 per double room per night, breakfast included • Debit/credit card; cheques/cash accepted
Open:	Year round
Description:	Large, Victorian building overlooking Princess Gardens and close to the harbour. Big ballroom with entertainment provided every night.
Facilities:	
To Beach:	0.44 miles

TORQUAY – CORBYN HEAD (TORRE ABBEY)

Torcroft Hotel ★★Hotel

28-30 Croft Road, Torquay, Devon, TQ2 5UE

T:	+44 (0) 1803 298292
E:	enquiries@torcroft.co.uk
W:	torcroft.co.uk
Bedrooms:	15 • £54.00-£74.00 per double room per night, breakfast included • Debit/credit card; cheques/cash accepted
Open:	Year round
Description:	Elegant Victorian villa set in its own grounds. Ample parking. Close to sea front and town centre. Home-cooked food.
Facilities:	
To Beach:	0.29 miles

TORQUAY – CORBYN HEAD (TORRE ABBEY)

Tower Hall Hotel ★★★★Guest Accommodation

Solsbro Road, Torquay, Devon, TQ2 6PF

T: +44 (0) 1803 605292
E: johnbutler@towerhallhotel.co.uk
W: towerhallhotel.co.uk

Bedrooms: 11 • £34.00-£48.00 per double room per night, breakfast included • Cheques/cash accepted

Open: Year round except Christmas and New Year

Description: Family hotel within easy walking distance of beaches, gardens and entertainment. Large, Victorian house with sea views in peaceful area.

Facilities: P

To Beach: 0.33 miles

TORQUAY – CORBYN HEAD (TORRE ABBEY)

Trelawney Hotel ★★★★Guest Accommodation

48 Belgrave Road, Torquay, Devon, TQ2 5HS

T: +44 (0) 1803 296049
E: trelawneyhotel@hotmail.com
W: trelawneyhotel.co.uk

Bedrooms: 12 • £40.00-£70.00 per double room per night, breakfast included • Debit/credit card; cheques/cash accepted

Open: Year round except Christmas

Description: Friendly, family-run, licensed hotel. Close to main shops, beaches, theatres, conference/leisure centre. A warm welcome always guaranteed. Highly recommended.

Facilities:

To Beach: 0.3 miles

TORQUAY – CORBYN HEAD (TORRE ABBEY)

Villa Oasis Guesthouse ★★★Guest Accommodation

21 Newton Road, Torquay, Devon, TQ2 5DB

T: +44 (0) 1803 297404
E: infovillaoasis@aol.com
W: villa-oasis.co.uk

Bedrooms: 7 • £42.00-£48.00 per double room per night, breakfast included • Debit/credit card; cheques/cash accepted

Open: Seasonal opening – call for details

Description: Villa Oasis is a "child-free" B&B for the comfort of its guests, allowing them to relax in the lounge or on the large, decked, games patio.

Facilities: P

To Beach: 0.77 miles

TORQUAY – CORBYN HEAD (TORRE ABBEY)

Walnut Lodge ★★★★Guest Accommodation

48 Bampfylde Road, Torquay, Devon, TQ2 5AY

T:	+44 (0) 1803 200471
E:	walnutlodge@msn.com
W:	walnutlodgeTorquay.co.uk
Bedrooms:	5 • £40.00-£50.00 per double room per night, breakfast included • Debit/credit card accepted
Open:	Year round
Description:	An elegant Victorian guesthouse set in an ideal location. There are five beautiful en suite rooms and a private car park.
Facilities:	[facility symbols]
To Beach:	0.32 miles

TORQUAY – CORBYN HEAD (TORRE ABBEY)

Westbourne Hotel ★★★★Guest Accommodation

106 Avenue Road, Torquay, Devon, TQ2 5LQ

T:	+44 (0) 1803 292927
E:	enquiries@westbournehotelTorquay.co.uk
W:	westbournehotelTorquay.co.uk
Bedrooms:	7 • £50.00-£70.00 per double room per night, breakfast included • Debit/credit card; cheques/cash accepted
Open:	Year round except Christmas and New Year
Description:	The Westbourne Hotel is, in the words of its owners, "alive with fresh thinking" and new ideas. It has central heating, heated pool, sun terrace, car park and is non-smoking.
Facilities:	[facility symbols]
To Beach:	0.67 miles

TORQUAY – CORBYN HEAD (TORRE ABBEY)

Westbrook Hotel ♦♦♦Guest Accommodation

15 Scarborough Road, Torquay, Devon, TQ2 5UJ

T:	+44 (0) 1803 292559
E:	westbrookhotel@tesco.net
W:	westbrookhotel.net
Bedrooms:	6 • £42.00-£47.00 per double room per night, breakfast included • Debit/credit card accepted
Open:	Year round except New Year
Description:	The Westbrook is a small, family-run hotel in the centre of Torquay, aiming to give good quality and service.
Facilities:	[facility symbols]
To Beach:	0.26 miles

TORQUAY – HOLLACOMBE BEACH

Corbyn Head Hotel

★★★Hotel

Torbay Road, The Sea Front, Torquay, Devon, TQ2 6RH

SILVER AWARD

T: +44 (0) 1803 213611
E: arew@corbynhead.com
W: corbynhead.com

Bedrooms: 45 • £70.00-£300.00 per double room per night, breakfast included • Debit/credit card; cheques/cash accepted

Open: Year round

Description: An exclusive hotel set on Torquay seafront with panoramic views of Torbay and with two award-winning restaurants.

Facilities:

To Beach: 0.5 miles

TORQUAY – HOLLACOMBE BEACH

Livermead Cliff Hotel

★★★Hotel

Torbay Road, Torquay, Devon, TQ2 6RQ

T: +44 (0) 1803 299666
E: enquiries@livermeadcliff.co.uk
W: livermeadcliff.co.uk

Bedrooms: 67 • £79.00-£150.00 per double room per night, breakfast included • Debit/credit card; cheques/cash accepted

Open: Year round

Description: Situated at the water's edge in a secluded garden, with magnificent views over Torbay. Family-owned and run. Ample car parking.

Facilities:

To Beach: 0.5 miles

TORQUAY – MEADFOOT BEACH

Cary Court Hotel

♦♦♦♦Guest Accommodation

Hunsdon Road, Torquay, Devon, TQ1 1QB

T: +44 (0) 1803 209205
E: stay@carycourthotel.co.uk
W: carycourthotel.co.uk

Bedrooms: 12 • £50.00-£75.00 per double room per night, breakfast included • Debit/credit card; cheques/cash accepted

Open: Seasonal opening – call for details

Description: A plantation-style house with elegant style and charm, Cary Court invites you to spoil yourself by paying a visit.

Facilities:

To Beach: 0.63 miles

TORQUAY – MEADFOOT BEACH

Clevedon Hotel ♦♦♦♦Guest Accommodation

Meadfoot Sea Road, Torquay, Devon, TQ1 2LQ

T:	+44 (0) 1803 294260
E:	enquiries@clevedonhotel.co.uk
W:	clevedonhotel.co.uk
Bedrooms:	10 • £50.00-£80.00 per double room per night, breakfast included • Debit/credit card accepted
Open:	Year round
Description:	Elegant, licensed, family-run, detached, Victorian residence close to beach and shops. Relaxing atmosphere, personal service and car parking.
Facilities:	[symbols]
To Beach:	0.34 miles

TORQUAY – MEADFOOT BEACH

Frognel Hall Hotel ★★Hotel

Higher Woodfield Road, Torquay, Devon, TQ1 2LD

T:	+44 (0) 1803 298339
E:	mail@frognel.co.uk
W:	frognel.co.uk
Bedrooms:	27 • £40.00-£70.00 per double room per night, breakfast included • Debit/credit card; cheques/cash accepted
Open:	Year round
Description:	Beautiful Listed mansion set in two acres of peaceful gardens. Close to harbour, town centre and beaches. Ample parking, great views across the bay.
Facilities:	[symbols]
To Beach:	0.38 miles

TORQUAY – MEADFOOT BEACH

Osborne Hotel ★★★★Hotel

Hesketh Crescent, Meadfoot Beach, Torquay, Devon, TQ1 2LL SILVER AWARD

T:	+44 (0) 1803 213311
E:	enq@osborne-Torquay.co.uk
W:	osborne-Torquay.co.uk
Bedrooms:	32 • £120.00-£236.00 per double room per night, breakfast included • Debit/credit card; cheques/cash accepted
Open:	Year round
Description:	Located in a Regency crescent overlooking Torbay. Offers affordable elegance. Award-winning restaurant. Extensive grounds and facilities plus a warm, friendly atmosphere.
Facilities:	[symbols]
To Beach:	0.15 miles

TORQUAY – MEADFOOT BEACH

Shirley Hotel ★★★B&B

Braddons Hill Road East, Torquay, Devon, TQ1 1HF

T: +44 (0) 1803 293016
E: enquiries@shirley-hotel.co.uk
W: shirley-hotel.co.uk

Bedrooms: 12 • £50.00-£58.00 per double room per night, breakfast included • Debit/credit card; cheques/cash accepted

Open: Year round except Christmas and New Year

Description: Friendly, family-run hotel quietly situated yet close to harbour, shops and restaurants. Outdoor pool, relaxing sauna and Jacuzzi.

Facilities:

To Beach: 0.5 miles

TORQUAY – MEADFOOT BEACH

The Somerville Hotel ♦♦♦♦Guest Accommodation

515 Babbacombe Road, Torquay, Devon, TQ1 1HJ

T: +44 (0) 1803 294755
E: stay@somervillehotel.co.uk
W: somervillehotel.co.uk

Bedrooms: 11 • £52.00-£80.00 per double room per night, breakfast included • Debit/credit card accepted

Open: Year round except Christmas

Description: Conveniently located for town harbour, this Victorian villa stands in its own grounds. Ample parking with a warm and friendly welcome assured.

Facilities:

To Beach: 0.5 miles

TORQUAY – ODDICOMBE BEACH

Anchorage Hotel ★★Hotel

Aveland Road, Torquay, Devon, TQ1 3PT

T: +44 (0) 1803 326175
E: enquiries@anchoragehotel.co.uk
W: anchoragehotel.co.uk

Bedrooms: 56 • £45.00-£89.00 per double room per night, breakfast included • Debit/credit card; cheques/cash accepted

Open: Year round

Description: Situated 800 yards level walk from downs, seafront, and shops. Adjacent to bowling green and tennis courts. Quiet parkland setting. Family-owned and run.

Facilities:

To Beach: 0.5 miles

TORQUAY – ODDICOMBE BEACH

Avron House ♦♦♦Guest Accommodation

70 Windsor Road, Ellacombe, Torquay, Devon, TQ1 1SZ

T:	+44 (0) 1803 294182
E:	stay@avronhotelTorquay.co.uk
W:	avronhotelTorquay.co.uk
Bedrooms:	10 • £40.00-£56.00 per double room per night, breakfast included • Debit/credit card; cheques/cash accepted
Open:	Year round except Christmas and New Year
Description:	A guesthouse with single, twin, double and family rooms. Situated between Babbacombe and Torquay centre.
Facilities:	[symbols]
To Beach:	0.78 miles

TORQUAY – ODDICOMBE BEACH

Babbacombe Palms ★★★Guest Accommodation

2 York Road, Babbacombe, Torquay, Devon, TQ1 3SG

T:	+44 (0) 1803 327087
E:	reception@babbacombepalms.com
W:	babbacombepalms.com
Bedrooms:	9 • £40.00-£60.00 per double room per night, breakfast included
Open:	Year round
Description:	The Babbacombe Palms is a licensed guesthouse offering clean, comfortable accommodation close to the beautiful Babbacombe Downs and beaches.
Facilities:	[symbols]
To Beach:	0.26 miles

TORQUAY – ODDICOMBE BEACH

Exmouth View Hotel ★★Hotel

St Albans Road, Babbacombe, Torquay, Devon, TQ1 3LG

T:	+44 (0) 1803 327307
E:	relax@exmouth-view.co.uk
W:	exmouth-view.co.uk
Bedrooms:	26 • £50.00-£60.00 per double room per night, breakfast included • Debit/credit card; cheques/cash accepted
Open:	Year round
Description:	A modern, detached hotel in one of the finest positions, close to the stunning Babbacombe Downs, St Marychurch Shopping Precinct, beaches, theatre, model village, Cliff Railway and Bygones.
Facilities:	P[symbols]
To Beach:	0.22 miles

TORQUAY – ODDICOMBE BEACH

Seabury Hotel ★★★★Guest Accommodation

Manor Road, Babbacombe, Torquay, Devon, TQ1 3JX

T:	+44 (0) 1803 327255
E:	enquiries@seaburyhotel.co.uk
W:	seaburyhotel.co.uk
Bedrooms:	23 • £40.00-£52.00 per double room per night, breakfast included • Debit/credit card; cheques/cash accepted
Open:	Seasonal opening – call for details
Description:	A family-run, licensed hotel set in its own grounds close to the beautiful Babbacombe Downs, beaches and local amenities.
Facilities:	
To Beach:	0.39 miles

TORQUAY – ODDICOMBE BEACH

Trecarn Hotel ♦♦♦Guest Accommodation

Palermo Road, Torquay, Devon, TQ1 3NW

T:	+44 (0) 1803 329292
E:	reservations@washearings.com
W:	washearings.com
Bedrooms:	134 • £25.00-£48.00 per double room per night, room only • Debit/credit card accepted
Open:	Year round
Description:	A delightful hotel in a peaceful location, the Trecarn is only a stroll to Babbacombe Downs, overlooking the bay.
Facilities:	P
To Beach:	0.34 miles

WOOLACOMBE – WOOLACOMBE SANDS

Golden Coast Holiday Village ★★★★Holiday Park

Station Road, Woolacombe, Devon, EX34 7HW

T:	+44 (0) 1271 870343
E:	goodtimes@woolacombe.com
W:	woolacombe.com
Pitches:	622 • £12.50-£45.00 per caravan per night • Debit/credit card; cheques/cash accepted
Open:	Seasonal opening – call for details
Description:	Lively park in picturesque setting close to beach. Free use of four holiday park facilities. Superb selection of accommodation.
Facilities:	P
To Beach:	1.6 miles

WOOLACOMBE – WOOLACOMBE SANDS

Ossaborough House ♦♦♦♦Guest Accommodation

Ossaborough Lane, Woolacombe, Devon, EX34 7HJ

T:	+44 (0) 1271 870297
E:	info@ossaboroughhouse.co.uk
W:	ossaboroughhouse.co.uk
Bedrooms:	6 • £64.00-£82.00 per double room per night, breakfast included • Debit/credit card accepted
Open:	Year round except Christmas and New Year
Description:	A 17thC former farmhouse, situated in countryside, close to beach. Quiet and peaceful.
Facilities:	
To Beach:	1.71 miles

WOOLACOMBE – WOOLACOMBE SANDS

The Narracott Hotel ★★Hotel

Beach Road, Woolacombe, Devon, EX34 7BS

T:	+44 (0) 1271 870418
E:	enquiries@narracott.co.uk
W:	narracott.co.uk
Bedrooms:	79 • £68.00-£124.00 per double room per night, breakfast included • Debit/credit card; cheques/cash accepted
Open:	Seasonal opening – call for details
Description:	A superbly situated seafront hotel with extensive leisure facilities. Ideal for family holidays, breaks and large parties.
Facilities:	
To Beach:	0.8 miles

WOOLACOMBE – WOOLACOMBE SANDS

Woolacombe Bay Hotel ★★★Hotel

Woolacombe, Devon, EX34 7BN — SILVER AWARD

T:	+44 (0) 1271 870388
E:	woolacombe.bayhotel@btinternet.com
W:	woolacombe-bay-hotel.co.uk
Bedrooms:	62 • £130.00-£140.00 per double room per night, breakfast included • Debit/credit card; cheques/cash accepted
Open:	Seasonal opening – call for details
Description:	Gracious hotel in six acres of grounds by Blue Flag golden sands. Extensive, free sporting facilities and creche provided while you play. Excellent cuisine, fine wines.
Facilities:	
To Beach:	0.7 miles

BEACON HILL – ROCKLEY SANDS

Beacon Hill Touring Park ★★Camping & Touring Park

Blandford Road North, Beacon Hill, Nr Lytchett Minster, Poole, Dorset, BH16 6AB

T:	+44 (0) 1202 631631
E:	bookings@beaconhilltouringpark.co.uk
W:	beaconhilltouringpark.co.uk
Pitches:	220 • £11.50-£23.00 per caravan per night
Open:	Seasonal opening – call for details
Description:	The park covers some 30 acres of wooded heathland with open grassy spaces and two small lakes. Set at the foot of Beacon Hill, a local beauty spot and view point for Poole, its harbour and Purbecks.
Facilities:	
To Beach:	1.91 miles

BOURNEMOUTH – ALUM CHINE BEACH

Golden Sovereign Hotel ♦♦♦♦Guest Accommodation

97 Alumhurst Road, Bournemouth, Dorset, BH4 8HR

T:	+44 (0) 1202 762088
E:	scott.p@talk21.com
W:	goldensovereignhotel.com
Bedrooms:	9 • £40.00-£60.00 per double room per night, breakfast included • Debit/credit card; cheques/cash accepted
Open:	Year round except New Year
Description:	A Victorian, character hotel. Beach and wooded walks nearby. Regency-style dining-room with traditional menus. Non-smoking bedrooms, smoking in bar only.
Facilities:	
To Beach:	0.32 miles

BOURNEMOUTH – ALUM CHINE BEACH

Riviera Hotel ★★★Hotel

14-16 Burnaby Road, Alum Chine, Bournemouth, Dorset, BH4 8JF

T:	+44 (0) 1202 763653
E:	info@rivierabournemouth.co.uk
W:	rivierabournemouth.co.uk
Bedrooms:	73 • £70.00-£140.00 per double room per night, breakfast included • Debit/credit card; cheques/cash accepted
Open:	Year round
Description:	Situated in the beautiful wooded area of Alum Chine with views across the bay to the Isle of Wight.
Facilities:	
To Beach:	0.26 miles

DORSET

BOURNEMOUTH – ALUM CHINE BEACH

Southernhay Hotel
★★★Guest Accommodation

42 Alum Chine Road, Westbourne, Bournemouth, Dorset, BH4 8DX

T:	+44 (0) 1202 761251
E:	enquiries@southernhayhotel.co.uk
W:	southernhayhotel.co.uk
Bedrooms:	6 • £40.00-£56.00 per double room per night, breakfast included • Cheques/cash accepted
Open:	Year round
Description:	High standard accommodation, near beach, restaurants and shops. Full English and vegetarian breakfast, rooms with colour TV, radio alarms, hairdryers and tea-/coffee-making facilities. Large car park.
Facilities:	
To Beach:	0.67 miles

BOURNEMOUTH – BOSCOMBE PIER BEACH

Balincourt Hotel
★★★★★Guesthouse

58 Christchurch Road, Bournemouth, Dorset, BH1 3PF SILVER AWARD

T:	+44 (0) 1202 552962
E:	rooms@balincourt.co.uk
W:	balincourt.co.uk
Bedrooms:	10 • £74.00-£80.00 per double room per night, breakfast included • Debit/credit card; cheques/cash accepted
Open:	Year round except Christmas
Description:	Balincourt is a non-smoking, friendly hotel. All rooms individually decorated, old-fashioned hospitality and traditional home cooking.
Facilities:	
To Beach:	0.47 miles

BOURNEMOUTH – BOSCOMBE PIER BEACH

Best Western Chine Hotel
★★★Hotel

Boscombe Spa Road, Bournemouth, Dorset, BH5 1AX

T:	+44 (0) 1202 396234
E:	reservations@chinehotel.co.uk
W:	chinehotel.co.uk
Bedrooms:	86 • £110.00-£210.00 per double room per night, breakfast included • Debit/credit card; cheques/cash accepted
Open:	Year round
Description:	An attractive, Victorian hotel, quietly located and set in three acres of mature gardens. There is direct access to the beach via a pine-fringed walkway.
Facilities:	
To Beach:	0.15 miles

BOURNEMOUTH – BOSCOMBE PIER BEACH

Cransley Hotel ★★★★Guest Accommodation

11 Knyveton Road, East Cliff, Bournemouth, Dorset, BH1 3QG

T: +44 (0) 1202 290067
E: info@cransley.com
W: cransley.com

Bedrooms: 11 • £60.00-£70.00 per double room per night, breakfast included • Debit/credit card; cheques/cash accepted

Open: Year round except Christmas

Description: Set in pleasant grounds in pine tree avenue. Close to East Cliff and all amenities. High standards and warm welcome assured.

Facilities:

To Beach: 0.72 miles

BOURNEMOUTH – BOSCOMBE PIER BEACH

Denewood Hotel ★★★Guest Accommodation

1 Percy Road, Bournemouth, Dorset, BH5 1JE

T: +44 (0) 1202 394493
E: info@denewood.co.uk
W: denewood.co.uk

Bedrooms: 10 • £45.00-£60.00 per double room per night, breakfast included • Debit/credit card; cheques/cash accepted

Open: Year round except Christmas and New Year

Description: Small, family hotel by the sea, with its own beauty salon. Central to amenities and beach.

Facilities: P

To Beach: 0.28 miles

BOURNEMOUTH – BOSCOMBE PIER BEACH

Majestic Hotel ♦♦♦♦Guest Accommodation

34 Derby Road, East Cliff, Bournemouth, Dorset, BH1 3QE

T: +44 (0) 1942 824824
E: reservations@washearings.com
W: washearings.com

Bedrooms: 69 • £52.00-£92.00 per double room per night, breakfast included • Debit/credit card; cheques/cash accepted

Open: Year round

Description: Purpose-built 1930s hotel. Large public areas on ground floors, ballroom/bar, dining room, TV and games room. Sun patio and outside pool from May to September. All rooms are en suite. Lift serves all three floors.

Facilities: P

To Beach: 0.5 miles

BOURNEMOUTH – BOSCOMBE PIER BEACH

Ocean View Hotel ★★★Hotel

East Overcliff Drive, Bournemouth, Dorset, BH1 3AR

T: +44 (0) 1202 558057
E: enquiry@oceanview.uk.com
W: oceanview.uk.com

Bedrooms: 52 • £176.00-£352.00 per double room per night, breakfast included • Debit/credit card accepted

Open: Year round

Description: On the East Cliff, facing the sea. Bournemouth's main shopping centre is close by. Good service and personal attention. Dancing during the season and some weekends. Recently refurbished function suites and bedrooms.

Facilities:

To Beach: 0.73 miles

BOURNEMOUTH – BOSCOMBE PIER BEACH

Wenrose ♦♦♦Guest Accommodation

23 Drummond Road, Boscombe, Bournemouth, Dorset, BH1 4DP

T: +44 (0) 1202 396451
E: wenrose@bigfoot.com
W: bournemouthbedandbreakfast.com

Bedrooms: 4 • £25.00 per double room per night, breakfast included

Open: Year round except Christmas and New Year

Description: Victorian house which is close to shops, sea and public transport. Facilities include en suite bathroom and broadband access. Ideal for business people. Opened in January 2005. A non-smoking establishment.

Facilities:

To Beach: 0.41 miles

BOURNEMOUTH – B'MOUTH PIER BEACH

Belvedere Hotel ★★★Hotel

Bath Road, Bournemouth, Dorset, BH1 2EU

T: +44 (0) 1202 293336
E: enquiries@belvedere-hotel.co.uk
W: belvedere-hotel.co.uk

Bedrooms: 100 • £60.00-£120.00 per double room per night, breakfast included • Debit/credit card; cheques/cash accepted

Open: Year round

Description: Centrally situated for beach, shops, town, conference venues and theatres. Personally supervised by proprietors with good food, entertainment and friendly service.

Facilities:

To Beach: 0.32 miles

BOURNEMOUTH – B'MOUTH PIER BEACH

The Hermitage Hotel
★★★Hotel
SILVER AWARD

Exeter Road, Bournemouth, Dorset, BH2 5AH

T:	+44 (0) 1202 557363
E:	info@hermitage-hotel.co.uk
W:	hermitage-hotel.co.uk
Bedrooms:	75 • £90.00-£128.00 per double room per night, breakfast included • Debit/credit card; cheques/cash accepted
Open:	Year round
Description:	Undeniably one of the best located hotels in Bournemouth, situated directly opposite the Pier, Central Gardens and BIC Conference Centre.
Facilities:	[facility symbols]
To Beach:	0.12 miles

BOURNEMOUTH – DURLEY CHINE BEACH

Best Western Connaught Hotel
★★★Hotel

West Hill Road, West Cliff, Bournemouth, Dorset, BH2 5PH

T:	+44 (0) 1202 298020
E:	sales@theconnaught.co.uk
W:	theconnaught.co.uk
Bedrooms:	56 • £88.00-£158.00 per double room per night, breakfast included • Debit/credit card; cheques/cash accepted
Open:	Year round
Description:	Hotel ideally situated five minutes' walk from conference/leisure centre, beach and pier. It has an indoor leisure centre, outdoor pool, beauty salon, two bars, two lounges, entertainment and car park.
Facilities:	[facility symbols]
To Beach:	0.17 miles

BOURNEMOUTH – DURLEY CHINE BEACH

Bonnington Hotel
♦♦♦Guest Accommodation

Tregonwell Road, Bournemouth, Dorset, BH2 5NT

T:	+44 (0) 1202 553621
E:	john@thebonningtonhotel.com
W:	thebonningtonhotel.com
Bedrooms:	20 • £50.00-£80.00 per double room per night, breakfast included • Debit/credit card; cheques/cash accepted
Open:	Year round
Description:	Friendly hotel in central Bournemouth, a short stroll from beach, conference centre and shops. Choice of menu. Licensed, cosy bar.
Facilities:	[facility symbols]
To Beach:	0.26 miles

BOURNEMOUTH – DURLEY CHINE BEACH

Cavendish

★★★★Guest Accommodation

20 Durley Chine Road, West Cliff, Bournemouth, Dorset, BH2 5LF

T:	+44 (0) 1202 290489
E:	info@cavendishhotel.uk.net
W:	cavendishhotel.uk.net
Bedrooms:	16 • £40.00-£74.00 per double room per night, breakfast included • Debit/credit card; cheques/cash accepted
Open:	Year round except Christmas and New Year
Description:	Family-owned house that offers offer high standard B&B accommodation with a relaxed and friendly atmosphere. No stag/hen parties!
Facilities:	
To Beach:	0.24 miles

BOURNEMOUTH – DURLEY CHINE BEACH

Hotel Riviera

★★Hotel

West Cliff Gardens, Bournemouth, Dorset, BH2 5HL

T:	+44 (0) 1202 552845
E:	info@hotel-riviera.co.uk
W:	hotel-riviera.co.uk
Bedrooms:	34 • £64.00-£80.00 per double room per night, breakfast included • Debit/credit card; cheques/cash accepted
Open:	Seasonal opening – call for details
Description:	The Hotel Riviera is on the West Cliff overlooking the sea, and has a garden with direct access to the cliff top.
Facilities:	P
To Beach:	0.06 miles

BOURNEMOUTH – DURLEY CHINE BEACH

Kiwi Hotel

★★Hotel

West Hill Road, Bournemouth, Dorset, BH2 5EG

T:	+44 (0) 1202 555889
E:	kiwihotel@aol.com
W:	kiwihotel.co.uk
Bedrooms:	47 • £56.00-£78.00 per double room per night, breakfast included • Debit/credit card; cheques/cash accepted
Open:	Year round
Description:	Family-run hotel 150 yards from cliff top and a few minutes from town centre. Choice of menu at all meals. Children welcome.
Facilities:	P
To Beach:	0.18 miles

BOURNEMOUTH – DURLEY CHINE BEACH

Redlands Hotel ★★★★Guest Accommodation

79 St Michaels Road, West Cliff, Bournemouth, Dorset, BH2 5DR

T: +44 (0) 1202 553714
E: enquiries@redlandshotel.co.uk
W: redlandshotel.co.uk

Bedrooms: 10 • £44.00-£72.00 per double room per night, breakfast included • Debit/credit card accepted

Open: Year round

Description: A small, family-run hotel near the beach, town centre, and Bournemouth International Centre, offering comfort and value.

Facilities:

To Beach: 0.25 miles

BOURNEMOUTH – DURLEY CHINE BEACH

Winter Dene Hotel ★★★★Guest Accommodation

11 Durley Road South, West Cliff, Bournemouth, Dorset, BH2 5JH

T: +44 (0) 1202 554150
E: info@winterdenehotel.com
W: winterdenehotel.com

Bedrooms: 13 • £66.00-£84.00 per double room per night, breakfast included • Debit/credit card; cheques/cash accepted

Open: Year round except Christmas

Description: Friendly, family-run hotel in large gardens close to beach and town centre. Excellent home cooking, licensed, car parking.

Facilities: P

To Beach: 0.17 miles

BOURNEMOUTH – FISHERMAN'S WALK

Alexander Lodge Hotel ★★★★Guesthouse

21 Southern Road, Southbourne, Bournemouth, Dorset, BH6 3SR

T: +44 (0) 1202 421662
E: alexanderlodge@yahoo.com
W: alexanderlodgehotel.co.uk

Bedrooms: 6 • £42.00-£62.00 per double room per night, breakfast included • Debit/credit card; cheques/cash accepted

Open: Year round except Christmas and New Year

Description: Delightful, small hotel, close to sea, shops and buses. Delicious home cooking, spotlessly clean en suite rooms and a warm welcome!

Facilities: P

To Beach: 0.6 miles

BOURNEMOUTH – FISHERMAN'S WALK

Beach Lodge ★★★★Guest Accommodation

61 Grand Avenue, Southbourne, Bournemouth, Dorset, BH6 3TA

T:	+44 (0) 1202 423396
E:	stay@beach-lodge.co.uk
W:	beach-lodge.co.uk
Bedrooms:	8 • £54.00-£68.00 per double room per night, breakfast included • Debit/credit card; cheques/cash accepted
Open:	Year round except Christmas and New Year
Description:	An Edwardian house sympathetically refurbished throughout, perfectly located two minutes' walk from Blue Flag beach and within walking distance of shops.
Facilities:	
To Beach:	0.68 miles

BOURNEMOUTH – FISHERMAN'S WALK

Fielden Court Hotel ★★★★Guesthouse

20 Southern Road, Bournemouth, Dorset, BH6 3SR

T:	+44 (0) 1202 427459
E:	enquiries@fieldencourthotel.co.uk
W:	fieldencourthotel.co.uk
Bedrooms:	8 • £50.00-£58.00 per double room per night, breakfast included • Debit/credit card; cheques/cash accepted
Open:	Year round
Description:	Relaxing, family-run hotel. All rooms en suite, with tea-/coffee-making facilities and TV. Three minutes' walk to cliff top, cliff lift and shops. Evening meal optional.
Facilities:	
To Beach:	0.62 miles

BOURNEMOUTH – FISHERMAN'S WALK

Mory House ★★★★Guest Accommodation

31 Grand Avenue, Southbourne, Bournemouth, Dorset, BH6 3SY SILVER AWARD

T:	+44 (0) 1202 433553
E:	stay@moryhouse.co.uk
W:	moryhouse.co.uk
Bedrooms:	6 • £60.00-£65.00 per double room per night, breakfast included
Open:	Year round except Christmas and New Year
Description:	Ideally situated just 200 yards from Southbourne's cliff top, this detached Victorian house provides six luxury en suite guest rooms.
Facilities:	
To Beach:	0.63 miles

BOURNEMOUTH – FISHERMAN'S WALK

Woodside Private Hotel ★★★★Guesthouse

29 Southern Road, Southbourne, Bournemouth, Dorset, BH6 3SR

T:	+44 (0) 1202 427213
E:	enquiries@woodsidehotel.co.uk
W:	woodsidehotel.co.uk
Bedrooms:	6 • £46.00-£56.00 per double room per night, breakfast included • Debit/credit card; cheques/cash accepted
Open:	Year round except New Year
Description:	Small, family-run, non-smoking establishment in a quiet road, a two-minute walk from a Blue Flag beach.
Facilities:	
To Beach:	0.6 miles

CHARMOUTH – CHARMOUTH WEST BEACH

Broadlands B&B ★★★B&B

Lower Sea Lane, Charmouth, Bridport, Dorset, DT6 6LR

T:	+44 (0) 1297 561181
E:	angela@bandbcharmouth.co.uk
W:	bandbcharmouth.co.uk/
Bedrooms:	1 • £60.00-£90.00 per double room per night, breakfast included • Debit/credit card accepted
Open:	Year round
Description:	Broadlands is a luxury, contemporary, en suite, self-contained B&B, 200 metres from the beach, with its own entrance and parking space. Dining area with integrated fridge and some self-catering facilities.
Facilities:	
To Beach:	0.19 miles

CHARMOUTH – CHARMOUTH WEST BEACH

Fernhill Hotel ★★Small Hotel

Fernhill, Charmouth, Bridport, Dorset, DT6 6BX

T:	+44 (0) 1297 560492
E:	mail@fernhill-hotel.co.uk
W:	fernhill-hotel.co.uk
Bedrooms:	12 • £110.00-£150.00 per double room per night, breakfast included • Debit/credit card accepted
Open:	Year round
Description:	Fernhill is somewhere you can enjoy the magnificent views, relax by the pool, eat fantastic, home-cooked food or indulge yourself with a relaxing treatment.
Facilities:	
To Beach:	0.98 miles

DORSET

CHARMOUTH – CHARMOUTH WEST BEACH

Hensleigh Hotel ★★Hotel

Lower Sea Lane, Charmouth, Bridport, Dorset, DT6 6LW

T:	+44 (0) 1297 560830
E:	info@hensleighhotel.co.uk
W:	hensleighhotel.co.uk
Bedrooms:	10 • £70.00-£120.00 per double room per night, breakfast included • Debit/credit card; cheques/cash accepted
Open:	Year round except Christmas and New Year
Description:	Comfortable, well-equipped, family-run hotel. Friendly atmosphere. Delicious food, local produce. Quiet position, close to sea and coastal walks.
Facilities:	
To Beach:	0.26 miles

CHARMOUTH – CHARMOUTH WEST BEACH

Manor Farm Holiday Centre

★★★Holiday, Touring & Camping Park

The Street, Charmouth, Bridport, Dorset, DT6 6QL

T:	+44 (0) 1297 560226
E:	enq@manorfarmholidaycentre.co.uk
W:	manorfarmholidaycentre.co.uk
Pitches:	689 • £9.00-£16.00 per caravan per night • Debit/credit card accepted
Open:	Year round
Description:	Large, open site in Area of Outstanding Natural Beauty close to the sea, from east end of Charmouth bypass. Come into Charmouth, site 0.75 miles on right.
Facilities:	
To Beach:	0.5 miles

CHARMOUTH – CHARMOUTH WEST BEACH

Queen's Armes Hotel ★★★★Guest Accommodation

The Street, Charmouth, Bridport, Dorset, DT6 6QF

T:	+44 (0) 1297 560339
E:	darkduck@btconnect.com
W:	queensarmeshotel.co.uk
Bedrooms:	10 • £64.00-£80.00 per double room per night, breakfast included • Debit/credit card accepted
Open:	Seasonal opening – call for details
Description:	Built as a manor-house for Forde Abbey about 1480. It retains many original features – oak walls, beams and stone fireplace.
Facilities:	
To Beach:	0.4 miles

CHARMOUTH – CHARMOUTH WEST BEACH

Wood Farm Caravan and Camping Park

★★★★★Holiday, Touring & Camping Park

Charmouth, Bridport, Dorset, DT6 6BT ROSE AWARD

T:	+44 (0) 1297 560697
E:	holidays@woodfarm.co.uk
W:	woodfarm.co.uk
Pitches:	220 • £10.50-£18.00 per motor caravan per night • Debit/credit card; cheques/cash accepted
Open:	Seasonal opening – call for details
Description:	Family-run park in rural West Dorset with breathtaking views and superb facilities.
Facilities:	
To Beach:	0.67 miles

LYME REGIS – CHARMOUTH WEST BEACH

Charnwood Guesthouse ♦♦♦♦Guest Accommodation

21 Woodmead Road, Lyme Regis, Dorset, DT7 3AD

T:	+44 (0) 1297 445281
E:	enquiries@lymeregisaccommodation.com
W:	lymeregisaccommodation.com
Bedrooms:	7 • £50.00-£60.00 per double room per night, breakfast included • Debit/credit card; cheques/cash accepted
Open:	Year round except Christmas
Description:	Edwardian guesthouse with en suite rooms and parking. Jurassic coastline and fossil hunting. Tour Dorset, Devon and Somerset. A comfortable base amid nature's splendour.
Facilities:	
To Beach:	1.53 miles

LYME REGIS – CHARMOUTH WEST BEACH

Clovelly Guesthouse ★★★★Guest Accommodation

View Road, Lyme Regis, Dorset, DT7 3AA SILVER AWARD

T:	+44 (0) 1297 444052
E:	clovelly@lymeregisbnb.com
W:	lymeregisbnb.com
Bedrooms:	3 • £52.00-£0.00 per double room per night, breakfast included • Cheques/cash accepted
Open:	Year round
Description:	Five minutes from sea and historic town of Lyme Regis. Spectacular sea and coastal views. All rooms en suite. Private parking.
Facilities:	
To Beach:	1.55 miles

LYME REGIS – CHARMOUTH WEST BEACH

Devonia Guesthouse ★★★★Guesthouse

2 Woodmead Road, Lyme Regis, Dorset, DT7 3AB

T: +44 (0) 1297 442869
E: roysue@fsmail.net.co.uk
W: devoniaguest.co.uk

Bedrooms: 4 • £20.00-£35.00 per double room per night, breakfast included • Debit/credit card; cheques/cash accepted

Open: Year round except Christmas

Description: Devonia offers comfortable, well-appointed accommodation in a small, family-run guesthouse. Views over Lyme Bay and rural views to the rear.

Facilities:

To Beach: 1.59 miles

LYME REGIS – CHARMOUTH WEST BEACH

Manaton ★★★★Guest Accommodation

Hill Road, Lyme Regis, Dorset, DT7 3PE

T: +44 (0) 1297 445138
E: enquiries@manaton.net
W: manaton.net

Bedrooms: 10 • £50.00-£60.00 per double room per night, breakfast included • Debit/credit card; cheques/cash accepted

Open: Year round except Christmas

Description: Friendly accommodation with a real home-from-home atmosphere. Great sea views and close to all town amenities. Private car park.

Facilities:

To Beach: 1.57 miles

LYME REGIS – CHARMOUTH WEST BEACH

Ocean View ★★★★Guest Accommodation

2 Hadleigh Villas, Silver Street, Lyme Regis, Dorset, DT7 3HR

T: +44 (0) 1297 442567
E: Jaybabe@supanet.com
W: lymeregis.com/ocean/view

Bedrooms: 3 • £48.00-£52.00 per double room per night, breakfast included • Cheques/cash accepted

Open: Seasonal opening – call for details

Description: Edwardian building sited some 200 yards from main street. Three letting rooms, all en suite. Home-from-home comforts in a family house.

Facilities:

To Beach: 1.6 miles

LYME REGIS – CHARMOUTH WEST BEACH

Old Lyme Guesthouse ★★★★Guesthouse

29 Coombe Street, Lyme Regis, Dorset, DT7 3PP GOLD AWARD

T:	+44 (0) 1297 442929
E:	oldlyme.guesthouse@virgin.net
W:	oldlymeguesthouse.co.uk
Bedrooms:	5 • £60.00-£64.00 per double room per night, breakfast included • Cheques/cash accepted
Open:	Year round
Description:	Historic 18thC building renovated and refurbished to a very high standard. Only three minutes' level walk to sea, shops and restaurants.
Facilities:	[facility symbols]
To Beach:	1.42 miles

LYME REGIS – CHARMOUTH WEST BEACH

Rotherfield ★★★★Guest Accommodation

View Road, Lyme Regis, Dorset, DT7 3AA

T:	+44 (0) 1297 445585
E:	rotherfield@lymeregis.com
W:	lymeregis.com/rotherfield/
Bedrooms:	6 • £50.00-£60.00 per double room per night, breakfast included • Cheques/cash accepted
Open:	Year round except Christmas
Description:	Clean, spacious and comfortable accommodation. Many rooms with sea views and only a few minutes' walk to the town and beach. Friendly atmosphere with full access to rooms all day. Private car park.
Facilities:	[facility symbols]
To Beach:	1.58 miles

LYME REGIS – CHARMOUTH WEST BEACH

Shamien House ★★★Guest Accommodation

8 Pound Street, Lyme Regis, Dorset, DT7 3HZ

T:	+44 (0) 1297 442339
E:	shamienhouse@btinternet.com
W:	shamienguesthouse.co.uk
Bedrooms:	6 • £54.00-£60.00 per double room per night, breakfast included • Debit/credit card accepted
Open:	Year round except Christmas
Description:	An historic house offering clean and comfortable en suite accommodation with a hearty breakfast. Central for town centre and beach.
Facilities:	[facility symbols]
To Beach:	1.61 miles

LYME REGIS – CHARMOUTH WEST BEACH

Springfield ♦♦♦♦Guest Accommodation

Woodmead Road, Lyme Regis, Dorset, DT7 3LJ

T:	+44 (0) 1297 443409
E:	springfield@lymeregis.com
W:	lymeregis.com/springfield
Bedrooms:	6 • £50.00-£60.00 per double room per night, breakfast included
Open:	Seasonal opening – call for details
Description:	Spacious Georgian house with comfortable rooms, most having views over Lyme Bay. Lovely conservatory and garden. Close to major footpaths.
Facilities:	[illegible]
To Beach:	1.62 miles

LYME REGIS – CHARMOUTH WEST BEACH

Thatch ♦♦♦♦Guest Accommodation

Uplyme Road, Lyme Regis, Dorset, DT7 3LP

T:	+44 (0) 1297 442212
E:	thatchbb@aol.com
W:	uk-bedandbreakfasts.co.uk
Bedrooms:	3 • £50.00-£58.00 per double room per night, breakfast included • Cheques/cash accepted
Open:	Year round
Description:	Very pretty, octagonal, thatched property. Sea and country views plus good food and comfortable beds. Safe parking.
Facilities:	[illegible]
To Beach:	1.78 miles

LYME REGIS – CHARMOUTH WEST BEACH

The London ★★★★Guest Accommodation

40 Church Street, Lyme Regis, Dorset, DT7 3DA

T:	+44 (0) 1297 442083
E:	info@londonlymeregis.co.uk
W:	londonlymeregis.co.uk
Bedrooms:	9 • £50.00-£65.00 per double room per night, breakfast included • Debit/credit card; cheques/cash accepted
Open:	Year round
Description:	Comfortable B&B accommodation in 17thC former coaching inn, two minutes' from Lyme seafront. Stunning cliff top and garden views. Ample parking.
Facilities:	P
To Beach:	1.32 miles

DORSET

LYME REGIS – CHARMOUTH WEST BEACH

The New Haven Hotel ★★★Guest Accommodation

1 Pound Street, Lyme Regis, Dorset, DT7 3HZ

T:	+44 (0) 1297 442499
E:	cherylnewhaven@hotmail.com
W:	lymeregishotels.co.uk
Bedrooms:	6 • £46.00-£70.00 per double room per night, breakfast included • Debit/credit card accepted
Open:	Year round
Description:	Charming accommodation in a 17thC townhouse having many period features. Ideal for town centre and seafront.
Facilities:	
To Beach:	1.63 miles

POOLE – HAMWORTHY PARK BEACH

Corkers Restaurant & Cafe Bar with Guest Rooms ★★★★Guesthouse

1 High Street, Poole, Dorset, BH15 1AB — SILVER AWARD

T:	+44 (0) 1202 681393
E:	corkers@corkers.co.uk
W:	corkers.co.uk/corkers
Bedrooms:	5 • £55.00-£65.00 per double room per night, breakfast included • Debit/credit card; cheques/cash accepted
Open:	Year round except New Year
Description:	Situated at the junction of High Street and Poole Quay, overlooking quayside. Cafe bar, restaurant and accommodation under one roof.
Facilities:	
To Beach:	0.77 miles

POOLE – HAMWORTHY PARK BEACH

Heathwood Guesthouse ◆◆◆◆Guest Accommodation

266 Wimborne Road, Oakdale, Poole, Dorset, BH15 3EF

T:	+44 (0) 1202 679176
E:	heathwoodhotel@tiscali.co.uk
W:	heathwoodhotel.co.uk
Bedrooms:	8 • £46.00-£66.00 per double room per night, breakfast included • Debit/credit card; cheques/cash accepted
Open:	Year round
Description:	Family-run, friendly atmosphere, satellite channels and TV in all rooms. Large breakfasts and evening meals. Close to Tower Park and Poole.
Facilities:	TV
To Beach:	1.95 miles

POOLE – LAKE PIER (HAM COMMON)

Sarnia Cherie

★★★★B&B

375 Blandford Road, Hamworthy, Poole, Dorset, BH15 4JL

T: +44 (0) 1202 679470
E: criscollier@aol.com
W: sarniacherie.co.uk

Bedrooms: 3 • £48.00-£50.00 per double room per night, breakfast included • Cheques/cash accepted

Open: Year round except Christmas

Description: A charming house only five minutes to Poole Quay, beaches and ferries. It has open views and safe parking. Ideal for exploring Dorset's coastline.

Facilities:

To Beach: 0.75 miles

POOLE – ROCKLEY SANDS

Rockley Park Holiday Park

★★★★★Holiday, Touring & Camping Park

Napier Road, Poole, Dorset, BH15 4LZ

T: +44 (0) 1202 679393
E: enquiries@british-holidays.co.uk
W: british-holidays.co.uk

Pitches: 416 • £22.00-£61.00 per caravan • Debit/credit card accepted

Open: Seasonal opening – call for details

Description: Complete seaside resort in one holiday park next to the beach, with direct access to boating launch. Facilities include cabarets, children's entertainers, sailing, adventure playground, indoor and outdoor pools, and table tennis.

Facilities: P

To Beach: 0.11 miles

POOLE – SANDBANKS PENINSULAR

Haven Hotel

★★★★Hotel

Banks Road, Sandbanks, Poole, Dorset, BH13 7QL

T: +44 (0) 1202 707333
E: reservations@havenhotel.co.uk
W: havenhotel.co.uk

Bedrooms: 78 • £198.00-£298.00 per double room per night, breakfast included • Debit/credit card; cheques/cash accepted

Open: Year round

Description: Located on the edge of the sea at the entrance to Poole Yacht Harbour, with views of the Purbeck Hills.

Facilities:

To Beach: 0.5 miles

SWANAGE – SWANAGE CENTRAL BEACH

Amberlea ★★★Guesthouse

36 Victoria Avenue, Swanage, Dorset, BH19 1AP

T:	+44 (0) 1929 426213
E:	stay@amberleahotel-swanage.co.uk
W:	amberleahotel-swanage.co.uk
Bedrooms:	5 • £44.00-£60.00 per double room per night, breakfast included
Open:	Year round
Description:	Small, family-run guesthouse, close to beach and town. All rooms en suite with colour TV and tea-/coffee-making facilities. Ample car parking.
Facilities:	P TV
To Beach:	0.3 miles

SWANAGE – SWANAGE CENTRAL BEACH

Bella Vista ♦♦♦♦Guest Accommodation

14 Burlington Road, Swanage, Dorset, BH19 1LS

T:	+44 (0) 1929 422873
E:	mail@bellavista-swanage.co.uk
W:	bellavista-swanage.co.uk
Bedrooms:	7 • £60.00-£80.00 per double room per night, breakfast included • Debit/credit card accepted
Open:	Seasonal opening – call for details
Description:	A stylish B&B with excellent facilities and wonderful sea views, directly overlooking Swanage Bay.
Facilities:	
To Beach:	0.5 miles

SWANAGE – SWANAGE CENTRAL BEACH

Cauldron Barn Farm Caravan Park

★★★★Holiday, Touring & Camping Park

Cauldron Barn Road, Swanage, Dorset, BH19 1QQ

T:	+44 (0) 1929 422080
E:	info@cauldronbarncaravanpark.co.uk
W:	dronbarncaravanpark.co.uk
Pitches:	42 • £12.00-£21.00 per caravan per night
Open:	Seasonal opening – call for details
Description:	Pleasant site set amid Purbeck Hills, 15 minutes' walk from main beach and town centre. Take main road to seafront, turn into Northbrook Road, then Cauldron Barn Road for park.
Facilities:	P
To Beach:	0.5 miles

SWANAGE – SWANAGE CENTRAL BEACH

Clare House

★★★★Guesthouse
1 Park Road, Swanage, Dorset, BH19 2AA
SILVER AWARD

T:	+44 (0) 1929 422855
E:	info@clare-house.com
W:	clare-house.com
Bedrooms:	6 • £60.00-£70.00 per double room per night, breakfast included • Debit/credit card accepted
Open:	Year round except Christmas
Description:	Lovely, home-from-home guesthouse 200 metres from sea and town centre close to Durlston Park and Heritage Coast.
Facilities:	
To Beach:	0.33 miles

SWANAGE – SWANAGE CENTRAL BEACH

Easter Cottage

♦♦♦♦Guest Accommodation
9 Eldon Terrace, Swanage, Dorset, BH19 1HA
SILVER AWARD

T:	+44 (0) 1929 427782
E:	daveanddiane@eastercottage.fsbusiness.co.uk
W:	eastercottage.co.uk
Bedrooms:	2 • £44.00-£60.00 per double room per night, breakfast included • Debit/credit card; cheques/cash accepted
Open:	Year round except Christmas
Description:	A 19thC Grade II Listed cottage on the level to beach and shops. Log fires in winter. Optional breakfast times.
Facilities:	
To Beach:	0.24 miles

SWANAGE – SWANAGE CENTRAL BEACH

Glenlee Hotel

★★★★Guesthouse
6 Cauldon Avenue, Swanage, Dorset, BH19 1PQ

T:	+44 (0) 1929 425794
E:	info@glenleehotel.co.uk
W:	glenleehotel.co.uk
Bedrooms:	6 • £50.00-£60.00 per double room per night, breakfast included • Debit/credit card accepted
Open:	Seasonal opening – call for details
Description:	Delightful position overlooking beach, gardens, bowling green and tennis courts. A short walk to beach. All rooms en suite with colour TV and hot drinks facilities.
Facilities:	P TV
To Beach:	0.31 miles

SWANAGE – SWANAGE CENTRAL BEACH

Grace Gardens Guesthouse

★★★★Guesthouse
SILVER AWARD

28 Victoria Avenue, Swanage, Dorset, BH19 1AP

T: +44 (0) 1929 422502
E: enquiries@gracegardens.co.uk
W: gracegardens.co.uk

Bedrooms: 5 • £46.00-£80.00 per double room per night, breakfast included

Open: Year round

Description: A friendly, family-run guesthouse. Ideally situated two minutes' flat walk from the sea, shops and bus station.

Facilities:

To Beach: 0.36 miles

SWANAGE – SWANAGE CENTRAL BEACH

Purbeck House Hotel

★★★Hotel

91 High Street, Swanage, Dorset, BH19 2LZ

T: +44 (0) 1929 422872
E: purbeckhouse@easynet.co.uk
W: purbeckhousehotel.co.uk

Bedrooms: 39 • £212.00 per double room per night, breakfast included • Debit/credit card; cheques/cash accepted

Open: Year round except Christmas

Description: Family-run hotel, set in 3.5 acres of gardens, 300 yards from beach. Off-street parking. Fully licensed.

Facilities:

To Beach: 0.28 miles

SWANAGE – SWANAGE CENTRAL BEACH

Swanage Haven

★★★Guesthouse

3 Victoria Road, Swanage, Dorset, BH19 1LY

T: +44 (0) 1929 423088
E: info@swanagehaven.com
W: swanagehaven.com

Bedrooms: 8 • £70.00-£80.00 per double room per night, breakfast included • Debit/credit card accepted

Open: Year round

Description: The Swanage Haven is just half a mile from the glorious sandy beach, and just minutes from Swanage town centre.

Facilities:

To Beach: 0.5 miles

SWANAGE – SWANAGE CENTRAL BEACH

Swanage YHA ★★★Hostel

Cluny Crescent, Swanage, Dorset, BH19 2BS

T:	+44 (0) 1929 422113
E:	swanage@yha.org.uk
W:	yha.org.uk
Bedrooms:	26 • £12.50-£19.00 per person per night, breakfast included • Debit/credit card; cheques/cash accepted
Open:	Seasonal opening – call for details
Description:	Elegant, Victorian house, overlooking Swanage Bay. Built on site of a monastery of the Cluny Order.
Facilities:	
To Beach:	0.41 miles

SWANAGE – SWANAGE CENTRAL BEACH

The Castleton Hotel ★★★★Guest Accommodation

1 Highcliffe Road, Swanage, Dorset, BH19 1LW — SILVER AWARD

T:	+44 (0) 1929 423972
E:	stay@castletonhotel-swanage.co.uk
W:	castletonhotel-swanage.co.uk
Bedrooms:	9 • £60.00-£79.00 per double room per night, breakfast included
Open:	Year round
Description:	A warm welcome awaits you along with a high standard of service, comfort and hospitality. Ideal base for Dorset coast.
Facilities:	
To Beach:	0.41 miles

SWANAGE – SWANAGE CENTRAL BEACH

The Limes Hotel ★★★★Guesthouse

48 Park Road, Swanage, Dorset, BH19 2AE

T:	+44 (0) 1929 422664
E:	info@limeshotel.net
W:	limeshotel.net
Bedrooms:	12 • £73.00 per double room per night, breakfast included • Debit/credit card; cheques/cash accepted
Open:	Year round
Description:	Small, informal hotel offering B&B all year round. Close to sea, town and wonderful walks. Families and pets welcome. Licensed bar. Private car park. Children over five are accommodated at greatly reduced rates.
Facilities:	
To Beach:	0.46 miles

SWANAGE – SWANAGE CENTRAL BEACH

The Pines Hotel ★★★Hotel

Burlington Road, Swanage, Dorset, BH19 1LT

T:	+44 (0) 1929 425211
E:	reservations@pineshotel.co.uk
W:	pineshotel.co.uk
Bedrooms:	43 • £113.00-£161.00 per double room per night, breakfast included • Debit/credit card; cheques/cash accepted
Open:	Year round
Description:	Family-run hotel set amid the Purbeck countryside at quiet end of Swanage Bay with its own access to beach.
Facilities:	[icons]
To Beach:	0.63 miles

SWANAGE – SWANAGE CENTRAL BEACH

Ulwell Cottage Caravan Park

★★★★Holiday, Touring & Camping Park

Ulwell, Swanage, Dorset, BH19 3DG

T:	+44 (0) 1929 422823
E:	enq@ulwellcottagepark.co.uk
W:	ulwellcottagepark.co.uk
Pitches:	294 • £14.00-£30.00 per caravan per night • Debit/credit card; cheques/cash accepted
Open:	Seasonal opening – call for details
Description:	Quiet site in picturesque setting adjoining Purbeck Hills. One-and-a-half miles from Swanage and two miles from Studland, the entrance is on the Swanage to Studland road.
Facilities:	[icons]
To Beach:	1.11 miles

UPTON – ROCKLEY SANDS

Tideway ★★★★B&B

Beach Road, Upton, Poole, Dorset, BH16 5NA

T:	+44 (0) 1202 621293
E:	tideway@tiscali.co.uk
W:	tidewaybb.co.uk
Bedrooms:	5 • £55.00-£60.00 per double room per night, room only • Cheques/cash accepted
Open:	Year round except Christmas and New Year
Description:	A peaceful, detached house that is modern, light and airy. Common areas include guest sitting room, breakfast room, conservatory, garden with spectacular views plus ample parking. Children accepted by arrangement. Non-smoking.
Facilities:	[icons]
To Beach:	1.22 miles

WEYMOUTH – WEYMOUTH CENTRAL

Anchorage Hotel ★★★★Guest Accommodation

7 The Esplanade, Weymouth, Dorset, DT4 8EB

T:	+44 (0) 1305 782542
E:	info@anchoragehotelweymouth.co.uk
W:	anchoragehotelweymouth.co.uk
Bedrooms:	8 • £48.00-£62.00 per double room per night, breakfast included • Debit/credit card accepted
Open:	Year round
Description:	A Grade II Listed building on the harbour affording panoramic views of Weymouth's bay. Rooms have full amenities.
Facilities:	
To Beach:	0.24 miles

WEYMOUTH – WEYMOUTH CENTRAL

Arcadia Guesthouse ★★★★Guest Accommodation

7 Waterloo Place, Weymouth, Dorset, DT4 7PA

T:	+44 (0) 1305 782458
E:	roywilcocks@hotmail.com
W:	arcadiaguesthouse.com
Bedrooms:	7 • £46.00-£66.00 per twin room per night, breakfast included • Debit/credit card; cheques/cash accepted
Open:	Year round except Christmas and New Year
Description:	Friendly, family-run, seafront guesthouse within walking distance of town and amenities. Families and groups welcome. Free car parking
Facilities:	P
To Beach:	0.44 miles

WEYMOUTH – WEYMOUTH CENTRAL

Beach View Guesthouse ★★★Guesthouse

3 The Esplanade, Weymouth, Dorset, DT4 8EA

T:	+44 (0) 1305 786528
E:	beachviewweymouth@hotmail.com
W:	beachviewguesthouse.com
Bedrooms:	6 • £50.00-£56.00 per double room per night, breakfast included • Debit/credit card accepted
Open:	Year round except Christmas
Description:	Family-run guesthouse on seafront. All rooms have either sea or harbour views.
Facilities:	P
To Beach:	0.25 miles

WEYMOUTH – WEYMOUTH CENTRAL

Cunard Guesthouse ★★★★Guest Accommodation

45-46 Lennox Street, Weymouth, Dorset, DT4 7HB

T:	+44 (0) 1305 771546
E:	stay@cunardguesthouse.co.uk
W:	cunardguesthouse.co.uk
Bedrooms:	8 • £44.00-£58.00 per double room per night, breakfast included • Debit/credit card accepted
Open:	Year round
Description:	The Cunard is a friendly, family-run establishment, just 100 yards from the seafront.
Facilities:	
To Beach:	0.43 miles

WEYMOUTH – WEYMOUTH CENTRAL

Eastney ★★★★Guest Accommodation

15 Longfield Road, Weymouth, Dorset, DT4 8RQ

T:	+44 (0) 1305 771682
E:	eastneyhotel@aol.com
W:	eastneyhotel.co.uk
Bedrooms:	10 • £50.00-£70.00 per double room per night, breakfast included • Debit/credit card; cheques/cash accepted
Open:	Year round except Christmas
Description:	Built around 1860, Victorian detached property in a third of an acre. Non-smoking establishment, close to wind surfing, sailing beaches.
Facilities:	
To Beach:	0.67 miles

WEYMOUTH – WEYMOUTH CENTRAL

Gloucester House ★★★Guest Accommodation

96 The Esplanade, Weymouth, Dorset, DT4 7AT

T:	+44 (0) 1305 785191
E:	gloucesterwey@aol.com
W:	gloucesterhouseweymouth.co.uk
Bedrooms:	14 • £50.00-£70.00 per double room per night, breakfast included • Debit/credit card; cheques/cash accepted
Open:	Year round
Description:	Gloucester House is on the Esplanade overlooking the bay. Central for shops, gardens and within 150 metres of bus and rail stations.
Facilities:	
To Beach:	0.17 miles

WEYMOUTH – WEYMOUTH CENTRAL

Harbour Lights ★★★★Guest Accommodation

20 Buxton Road, Weymouth, Dorset, DT4 9PJ

T: +44 (0) 1305 783273
E: harbourlights@btconnect.com
W: harbourlights-weymouth.co.uk

Bedrooms: 10 • £46.00-£54.00 per double room per night, breakfast included • Cheques/cash accepted

Open: Seasonal opening – call for details

Description: A Victorian house with magnificent views over Portland Harbour and the World Heritage coast. Ideally situated for exploring the area.

Facilities:

To Beach: 0.86 miles

WEYMOUTH – WEYMOUTH CENTRAL

Hotel Kinley ★★★Guest Accommodation

98 The Esplanade, Weymouth, Dorset, DT4 7AT

T: +44 (0) 1305 782264
E: hotelkinley@hotmail.com
W: hotelkinley.com

Bedrooms: 9 • £52.00-£76.00 per double room per night, breakfast included • Debit/credit card; cheques/cash accepted

Open: Year round

Description: Hotel on seafront and within easy reach of town centre. Own private garage. No seaview supplement.

Facilities:

To Beach: 0.17 miles

WEYMOUTH – WEYMOUTH CENTRAL

Hotel Prince Regent ★★★Hotel

139 The Esplanade, Weymouth, Dorset, DT4 7NR

T: +44 (0) 1305 771313
E: hprwey@aol.com
W: bestwestern.co.uk/hotel/083707.htm

Bedrooms: 70 • £65.00-£130.00 per double room per night, breakfast included • Debit/credit card; cheques/cash accepted

Open: Year round

Description: A warm welcome awaits at this refurbished Grade II Listed seafront hotel. Ideal for the business or leisure traveller.

Facilities:

To Beach: 0.4 miles

WEYMOUTH – WEYMOUTH CENTRAL

Hotel Rembrandt ★★★Hotel

12-18 Dorchester Road, Weymouth, Dorset, DT4 7JU

T:	+44 (0) 1305 764000
E:	reception@hotelrembrandt.co.uk
W:	hotelrembrandt.co.uk
Bedrooms:	78 • £80.00-£103.00 per double room per night, breakfast included • Debit/credit card; cheques/cash accepted
Open:	Year round
Description:	Weymouth's premier hotel, containing 78 spacious bedrooms, with 27 served by a lift. It has a leisure centre, one restaurant serving carvery/grill and coffee/snack bar.
Facilities:	[symbols]
To Beach:	0.72 miles

WEYMOUTH – WEYMOUTH CENTRAL

Hotel Rex ★★★Hotel

29 The Esplanade, Weymouth, Dorset, DT4 8DN

T:	+44 (0) 1305 760400
E:	rex@kingshotels.co.uk
W:	kingshotels.co.uk/rex.htm
Bedrooms:	31 • £80.00-£112.00 per double room per night, breakfast included • Debit/credit card; cheques/cash accepted
Open:	Year round except Christmas
Description:	Georgian townhouse on the Esplanade overlooking Weymouth Bay and adjacent to Pavilion. Close to harbour and town centre.
Facilities:	[symbols]
To Beach:	0.22 miles

WEYMOUTH – WEYMOUTH CENTRAL

Langham Hotel ★★★Guesthouse

130 The Esplanade, Weymouth, Dorset, DT4 7EX

T:	+44 (0) 1305 782530
E:	enquiries@langham-hotel.com
W:	langham-hotel.com
Bedrooms:	12 • £46.00-£62.00 per double room per night, breakfast included • Debit/credit card accepted
Open:	Year round except Christmas
Description:	Family-run seafront hotel with permit parking and residents' bar. All rooms are en suite with colour TV plus tea-/coffee-making facilities.
Facilities:	[symbols] TV
To Beach:	0.32 miles

WEYMOUTH – WEYMOUTH CENTRAL

Morven House Hotel ★★★★Guest Accommodation

2 Westerhall Road, Weymouth, Dorset, DT4 7SZ

T:	+44 (0) 1305 785075
E:	matthew.lambley@btinternet.com
W:	morvenweymouth.co.uk
Bedrooms:	9 • £50.00 per double room per night, breakfast included • Cheques/cash accepted
Open:	Seasonal opening – call for details
Description:	Small, family hotel, 150 yards from sea. Close to Greenhill Gardens and bird sanctuaries.
Facilities:	
To Beach:	0.61 miles

WEYMOUTH – WEYMOUTH CENTRAL

Oaklands Edwardian Guesthouse ★★★★Guest Accommodation

1 Glendinning Avenue, Weymouth, Dorset, DT4 7QF

T:	+44 (0) 1305 767081
E:	vicki@oaklands-guesthouse.co.uk
W:	oaklands-guesthouse.co.uk
Bedrooms:	8 • £42.00-£72.00 per double room per night, breakfast included • Debit/credit card; cheques/cash accepted
Open:	Year round except Christmas and New Year
Description:	An extensively refurbished Edwardian residence offering luxury B&B accommodation with the personal touch.
Facilities:	
To Beach:	0.63 miles

WEYMOUTH – WEYMOUTH CENTRAL

Pebble Bank Caravan Park ★★Holiday, Touring & Camping Park

90 Camp Road, Wyke Regis, Weymouth, Dorset, DT4 9HF

T:	+44 (0) 1305 774844
E:	info@pebblebank.co.uk
W:	pebblebank.co.uk
Pitches:	151 • £10.00-£14.00 per caravan per night • Debit/credit card; cheques/cash accepted
Open:	Seasonal opening – call for details
Description:	Quiet, family park in picturesque setting with superb sea views. Close to town centre.
Facilities:	
To Beach:	1.84 miles

WEYMOUTH – WEYMOUTH CENTRAL

Pebbles Guesthouse ★★★★Guest Accommodation

18 Kirtleton Avenue, Weymouth, Dorset, DT4 7PT

T:	+44 (0) 1305 784331
E:	info@pebblesguesthouse.co.uk
W:	pebblesguesthouse.co.uk
Bedrooms:	8 • £44.00-£55.00 per double room per night, breakfast included • Debit/credit card accepted
Open:	Year round
Description:	Family-run, Victorian guesthouse with private parking and garden. Convenient for the beach, town centre and station.
Facilities:	
To Beach:	0.65 miles

WEYMOUTH – WEYMOUTH CENTRAL

Spindrift Guesthouse ★★★Guest Accommodation

11 Brunswick Terrace, Weymouth, Dorset, DT4 7RW

T:	+44 (0) 1305 773625
E:	stay@spindriftguesthouse.co.uk
W:	spindriftguesthouse.co.uk
Bedrooms:	6 • £48.00-£64.00 per double room per night, breakfast included • Debit/credit card; cheques/cash accepted
Open:	Year round except Christmas
Description:	A friendly, family-run, non-smoking, Georgian-fronted guesthouse. Excellent seafront position with en suite rooms and TV in all bedrooms.
Facilities:	
To Beach:	0.46 miles

WEYMOUTH – WEYMOUTH CENTRAL

St John's Guesthouse ♦♦♦Guest Accommodation

7 Dorchester Road, Weymouth, Dorset, DT4 7JR

T:	+44 (0) 1305 775523
E:	stayat@stjohnsguesthouse.fsnet.co.uk
W:	stjohnsguesthouse.co.uk
Bedrooms:	8 • £44.00-£60.00 per double room per night, breakfast included • Debit/credit card accepted
Open:	Year round except Christmas and New Year
Description:	All rooms en suite. Large, free car park. Reduced rates for senior citizens and children over three years.
Facilities:	
To Beach:	0.5 miles

WEYMOUTH – WEYMOUTH CENTRAL

The Chatsworth ★★★★Guest Accommodation

14 The Esplanade, Weymouth, Dorset, DT4 8EB SILVER AWARD

T: +44 (0) 1305 785012
E: david@thechatsworth.co.uk
W: thechatsworth.co.uk

Bedrooms: 8 • £120.00-£200.00 per double room per night, breakfast included • Debit/credit card; cheques/cash accepted

Open: Year round

Description: Georgian terrace whose front rooms overlook seafront; rear overlook the harbour. Close to ferries. Quiet end of the Esplanade.

Facilities:

To Beach: 0.24 miles

WEYMOUTH – WEYMOUTH CENTRAL

The Redcliff ♦♦♦♦Guest Accommodation

18/19 Brunswick Terrace, Weymouth, Dorset, DT4 7RW

T: +44 (0) 1305 784682
E: contact@redcliffweymouth.co.uk
W: redcliffweymouth.co.uk

Bedrooms: 14 • £56.00-£72.00 per double room per night, breakfast included • Debit/credit card; cheques/cash accepted

Open: Year round except Christmas

Description: The Redcliff is a non-smoking, quality establishment just yards from the beach and Weymouth Bay.

Facilities:

To Beach: 0.46 miles

WEYMOUTH – WEYMOUTH CENTRAL

The Seaham ★★★★Guest Accommodation

3 Waterloo Place, Weymouth, Dorset, DT4 7NU GOLD AWARD

T: +44 (0) 1305 782010
E: stay@theseaham.co.uk
W: theseaham.co.uk

Bedrooms: 5 • £52.00-£70.00 per double room per night, breakfast included • Debit/credit card accepted

Open: Year round except Christmas

Description: Close to all amenities. All rooms are en suite with colour TV and beverage-making facilities. Choice of menu.

Facilities: TV

To Beach: 0.45 miles

WEYMOUTH – WEYMOUTH CENTRAL

Westwey Hotel ♦♦♦♦Guest Accommodation

62 Abbotsbury Road, Weymouth, Dorset, DT4 0BJ SILVER AWARD

T:	+44 (0) 1305 784564
E:	stay@westweyhotel.co.uk
W:	westweyhotel.co.uk
Bedrooms:	7 • £50.00-£75.00 per double room per night, breakfast included • Debit/credit card accepted
Open:	Year round
Description:	Situated within close walking distance of the beach and town centre. The Westway prides itself on the high standards throughout. All rooms are en suite. Strictly no smoking.
Facilities:	
To Beach:	0.5 miles

WEYMOUTH – WEYMOUTH CENTRAL

Weymouth Sands ★★★Guest Accommodation

5 The Esplanade, Weymouth, Dorset, DT4 8EA

T:	+44 (0) 1305 839022
E:	enquiries@weymouthsands.co.uk
W:	weymouthsands.co.uk
Bedrooms:	9 • £54.00-£64.00 per double room per night, breakfast included • Debit/credit card; cheques/cash accepted
Open:	Year round except Christmas and New Year
Description:	Georgian guesthouse on the seafront, with access to beach opposite front door. All bedrooms have either beach or harbour views.
Facilities:	
To Beach:	0.26 miles

WEYMOUTH – WEYMOUTH CENTRAL

Weyside Guesthouse ♦♦♦Guest Accommodation

1a Abbotsbury Road, Weymouth, Dorset, DT4 0AD

T:	+44 (0) 1305 772685
E:	weysideguesthouse@btinternet.com
W:	weysideguesthouse.btinternet.co.uk
Bedrooms:	4 • £50.00 per double room per night, breakfast included
Open:	Seasonal opening – call for details
Description:	A family establishment catering for same. Close to all attractions and the beach. All rooms have TV, wake-up alarm radio, hairdryers and are en suite; family rooms have bath and shower. Parking is limited.
Facilities:	TV
To Beach:	0.4 miles

HARTLEPOOL – SEATON CAREW

The Staincliffe Hotel ★★★Hotel

The Cliff, Seaton Carew, Hartlepool, TS25 1AB

T:	+44 (0) 1429 264301
E:	staincliffe@ukf.net
W:	thestaincliffe.com
Bedrooms:	20 • £140.00 per double room per night, breakfast included • Debit/credit card; cheques/cash accepted
Open:	Year round
Description:	Situated on the sea front, this hotel has individually designed theme rooms that surpass the highest expectations. A high reputation for food quality.
Facilities:	
To Beach:	0.73 miles

SEATON CAREW – FORESHORE

Norton Hotel ★★★Guest Accommodation

1a The Green, Seaton Carew, Hartlepool, TS25 1AR

T:	+44 (0) 1429 268317
E:	susanrusson@hotmail.com
W:	nortonhotel.co.uk
Bedrooms:	24 • £45.00 per double room per night, breakfast included • Debit/credit card accepted
Open:	Year round except Christmas and New Year
Description:	Enjoy staying in a bedroom with lovely sea views at the warm and friendly Norton Hotel.
Facilities:	
To Beach:	0.5 miles

DURHAM

HAYLING ISLAND – EASTOKE BEACH

Fishery Creek Caravan & Camping Park

★★★Camping & Touring Park

Fishery Lane, Hayling Island, Hampshire, PO11 9NR

T:	+44 (0) 23 9246 2164
E:	camping@fisherycreek.fsnet.co.uk
W:	keyparks.co.uk
Pitches:	495 • £10.00-£14.50 per caravan per night • Debit/credit card accepted
Open:	Seasonal opening – call for details
Description:	This touring site is at south-east Hayling, situated alongside a tidal creek with attractive views. It is within easy walking distance of the main beaches and two shopping areas.
Facilities:	
To Beach:	0.38 miles

HAMPSHIRE

HAMPSHIRE

HAYLING ISLAND – WEST BEACHLANDS

Seaventure ♦♦♦♦Guest Accommodation

20 Manor Way, Hayling Island, Hampshire, PO11 9JH

T:	+44 (0) 23 9234 6093
E:	patanddavids@tesco.net
W:	seaventure.co.uk
Bedrooms:	3 • £49.50-£55.00 per double room per night, breakfast included
Open:	Year round except Christmas and New Year
Description:	Small guesthouse just yards from beach. Tea-/coffee-making facilities, TV, video and fridge. Overnight storage for sail boards etc. Drying, wash down and freezer facilities.
Facilities:	
To Beach:	0.3 miles

ISLE OF WIGHT

BEMBRIDGE – ST HELENS BEACH

Flat 4 Highbury Court ★★★Self Catering

Lane End Road, Bembridge, Isle of Wight, PO35 5SU

T:	+44 (0) 13 9234 6093
E:	mail@bembridge-holiday-homes.co.uk
W:	islandvisitor.co.uk/bembridge.htm
Units:	1 • £200.00-£400.00 per unit per week
Open:	Seasonal opening – call for details
Description:	A spacious, self-contained, first floor apartment, sleeping four. Shared garden with outdoor pool. It is less than a quarter of a mile from Bembridge Lifeboat Station and the coast. Shops are 100 yards distant and the village centre is a 15-minute walk.
Facilities:	P
To Beach:	1.39 miles

BEMBRIDGE – ST HELENS BEACH

Whitecliff Bay Holiday Park ★★★★Holiday Park

Hillway Road, Bembridge, Isle of Wight, PO35 5PL

T:	+44 (0) 1983 872671
E:	holiday@whitecliff-bay.com
W:	whitecliff-bay.com
Pitches:	612 • £9.20-£23.40 per pitch, two people per night • Debit/credit card accepted
Open:	Seasonal opening – call for details
Description:	A family-owned and family-managed park which continues to promote great value, family holidays. Situated in a beautiful, rural location adjacent to its own secluded, sandy beach, it has facilities for all ages.
Facilities:	P
To Beach:	1.88 miles

COWES – WEST COWES BEACH

Anchorage Guesthouse ★★★★Guesthouse

23 Mill Hill Road, West Cowes, Isle of Wight, PO31 7EE

T:	+44 (0) 1983 247975
E:	peterandjenni@anchoragecowes.co.uk
W:	anchoragecowes.co.uk
Bedrooms:	4 • £50.00-£80.00 per double room per night, breakfast included
Open:	Year round
Description:	A small, friendly, family-run guesthouse offering residents' parking. Anchorage is convenient for marinas, waterfront and wide variety of restaurants and shops to be found in the charming, old town of Cowes.
Facilities:	[symbols]
To Beach:	0.64 miles

COWES – WEST COWES BEACH

Belharbour ★★★★★Self Catering

4 Egypt Copse, Egypt Hill, Cowes, PO31 8BA

T:	+44 (0) 20 8747 8308
E:	webmaster@belharbour.com
W:	belharbour.com
Units:	1 • £500.00-£1,300.00 per unit per week
Open:	Seasonal opening – call for details
Description:	A bright and spacious five-bedroom, luxury house in peaceful surroundings on Egypt Hill in West Cowes. Overlooking the Solent, it offers stunning sea views. It is a two-minute walk to the beach and a 12-minute stroll to Cowes itself.
Facilities:	[symbols]
To Beach:	0.33 miles

COWES – WEST COWES BEACH

New Holmwood Hotel ★★★Hotel

Queens Road, Egypt Point, West Cowes, PO31 8BW

T:	+44 (0) 1983 292508
E:	net@newholmwoodhotel.co.uk
W:	newholmwoodhotel.co.uk
Bedrooms:	26 • £96.00-£115.00 per double room per night, breakfast included • Debit/credit card accepted
Open:	Seasonal opening – call for details
Description:	The hotel not only offers the highest standards in terms of decor, comfort and food, but also its unique position on the water's edge at Egypt Point, provides unrivalled, panoramic views of the Solent.
Facilities:	[symbols]
To Beach:	0.19 miles

EAST COWES

Crossways House ★★★★Guest Accommodation

Crossways Road, East Cowes, Isle of Wight, PO32 6LJ SILVER AWARD

T: +44 (0) 1983 298282
E: enquiries@bedbreakfast-cowes.co.uk
W: bedbreakfast-cowes.co.uk

Bedrooms: 6 • £65.00-£75.00 per double room per night, breakfast included • Debit/credit card accepted

Open: Seasonal opening – call for details

Description: Crossways is just 100 yards from Osborne House and is close to the marinas at Cowes and East Cowes and the delightful village of Whippingham and Folly Reach. Quality, en suite accommodation.

Facilities:

To Beach: 1.11 miles

EAST COWES

Waverley Park ★★★★Holiday, Touring & Camping Park

51 Old Road, East Cowes, Isle of Wight, PO32 6AW

T: +44 (0) 1983 293452
E: holidays@waverley-park.co.uk
W: waverley-park.co.uk

Pitches: 118 • £8.00-£12.00 per caravan per night • Debit/credit card accepted

Open: Seasonal opening – call for details

Description: Waverley Park has access to the promenade east of the River Medina and enjoys panoramic views over Cowes Harbour and the Solent. Haven for wildlife especially red squirrels, ideal base for sailing, walking, cycling, fishing and golfing.

Facilities:

To Beach: 0.19 miles

FRESHWATER – COLWELL BAY

Heathfield Farm Camping Site

★★★★Camping & Touring Park

Heathfield Road, Freshwater, Isle of Wight, PO40 9SH

T: +44 (0) 1983 756756
E: web@heathfieldcamping.co.uk
W: heathfieldcamping.co.uk

Pitches: 60 • £8.50-£13.50 per caravan per night

Open: Seasonal opening – call for details

Description: Family camping in a quiet, rural area with magnificent sea and downland views. Located on the outskirts of Freshwater village, two miles from Yarmouth ferry port and the Needles.

Facilities:

To Beach: 0.38 miles

FRESHWATER – COLWELL BAY

Kings Lodge ★★★★★Self Catering

Kings Manor, Freshwater, Isle of Wight, PO40 9TL

T:	+44 (0) 1983 756756
E:	holidays@kingsmanorfarm.com
W:	kingsmanorfarm.co.uk
Units:	1 • £550.00-£1,950.00 per unit per week
Open:	Year round
Description:	Luxurious, stone farm lodge in grounds of manor house and organic farm overlooking the River Yar. Pool, stabling and tennis court. Beautiful setting with private courtyard. Walking distance to village, shops and beaches. Sleeps 10.
Facilities:	P
To Beach:	1.06 miles

FRESHWATER – COLWELL BAY

Seahorses ♦♦♦♦Guest Accommodation

Victoria Road, Freshwater, Isle of Wight, PO40 9PP

T:	+44 (0) 1983 752574
E:	seahorsesiow@lineone.net
W:	seahorsesisleofwight.com
Bedrooms:	4 • £50.00-£60.00 per double room per night, breakfast included
Open:	Seasonal opening – call for details
Description:	Seahorses offers comfortable B&B accommodation in large, en suite bedrooms. There are two family rooms, a double and a twin. Children and pets welcome.
Facilities:	P
To Beach:	1.17 miles

FRESHWATER – TOTLAND BEACH

Farringford Apartments ★★★Self Catering

Bedbury Lane, Freshwater, Isle of Wight, PO40 9PE

T:	+44 (0) 1983 753723
E:	enquiries@farringford.co.uk
W:	farringford.co.uk
Units:	29 • £287.00-£903.00 per unit per week • Debit/credit card accepted
Open:	Seasonal opening – call for details
Description:	Once the home of Alfred Lord Tennyson, the Farringford is in 33 acres of mature parkland. Spreading beyond the hotel's own grounds are 1,000 acres of National Trust downland. Within the grounds are the self-catering facilities.
Facilities:	P
To Beach:	1.23 miles

FRESHWATER – TOTLAND BEACH

Rockstone Cottage ♦♦♦♦Guest Accommodation

Colwell Chine Road, Colwell Bay, Freshwater, Isle of Wight, PO40 9NR

T:	+44 (0) 1983 753723
E:	nicky.drew@btopenworld.com
W:	rockstonecottage.co.uk
Bedrooms:	5 • £52.00 per double room per night, breakfast included
Open:	Seasonal opening – call for details
Description:	A charming cottage built in 1790, 300 yards from Colwell Bay and its safe, sandy beach. Surrounded by lovely walks and picturesque countryside, riding stables, golf course and leisure centre nearby.
Facilities:	
To Beach:	0.31 miles

NINHAM – SHANKLIN BEACH

Ninham Country Holidays ★★★Holiday & Touring Park

Ninham Farm, Shanklin, Isle of Wight, PO37 7PL

T:	+44 (0) 1983 864243
E:	info@ninham.fsnet.co.uk
W:	ninham-holidays.co.uk
Pitches:	94 • £12.00-£16.00 per motor caravan per night
Open:	Seasonal opening – call for details
Description:	Seaside enjoyment in a country lover's paradise. Luxury leisure homes (holiday caravans) in a peaceful country park setting overlooking wooded valley with small lakes. Next to island's premier resort and ideal base for touring.
Facilities:	P
To Beach:	1.03 miles

RYDE

Dorset House ★★★Guest Accommodation

31 Dover Street, Ryde, Isle of Wight, PO33 2BW

T:	+44 (0) 1983 564327
E:	hoteldorset@aol.com
W:	thedorsethotel.co.uk
Bedrooms:	23 • £47.00 per double room per night, breakfast included • Debit/credit card accepted
Open:	Year round except Christmas and New Year
Description:	Pleasantly situated two-three minutes from Ryde's six miles of sandy beaches and famous esplanade. Excellent shopping and a range of bars and restaurants are nearby, as are the rail, boat, hovercraft, bus and coach terminals.
Facilities:	P
To Beach:	0.61 miles

RYDE

Kasbah

★★★★Guest Accommodation

76 Union Street, Ryde, Isle of Wight, PO33 2LN

T: +44 (0) 1983 810088
E: newkasbah@btconnect.com
W: kas-bah.co.uk

Bedrooms: 9 • £70.00-£90.00 per double room per night, breakfast included • Debit/credit card accepted

Open: Seasonal opening – call for details

Description: Kasbah is a hidden treasure offering intimate boutique-style accommodation. Positioned a stone's throw away from Ryde seafront, the town and transport terminals – its location is ideal. Relax and unwind in the Moroccan cafe/bar.

Facilities:

To Beach: 0.84 miles

SANDOWN

Beaufort House

★★★Guest Accommodation

30 Broadway, Sandown, Isle of Wight, PO36 9BY

T: +44 (0) 1983 403672
E: enquiries@thebeaufortsandown.co.uk
W: thebeaufortsandown.co.uk

Bedrooms: 14 • £50.00-£70.00 per double room per night, breakfast included • Debit/credit card accepted

Open: Year round

Description: A friendly and informal, licensed, detached hotel – winner of two quality accolades for its hospitality and cleanliness. Ideally situated for beaches, shops, leisure centre, station, footpaths, gardens and cycleways.

Facilities: P

To Beach: 0.27 miles

SANDOWN

Burlington Hotel (Sandown)

★★Hotel

5-9 Avenue Road, Sandown, Isle of Wight, PO36 8BN

T: +44 (0) 1983 403702
E: burlingtonhotel.sandown@virgin.net
W: burlington-sandown.co.uk

Bedrooms: 68 • £56.00 per double room per night, breakfast included • Debit/credit card accepted

Open: Seasonal opening – call for details

Description: The Burlington is highly recommended for good food, comfort and for offering every facility for a relaxed and enjoyable holiday atmosphere. Two minutes from sandy beaches and all amenities.

Facilities: P

To Beach: 0.28 miles

SANDOWN

Chad Hill Hotel ★★Small Hotel

7 Hill Street, Sandown, Isle of Wight, PO36 9DD

T:	+44 (0) 1983 403231
E:	enquiries@chadhillhotel.co.uk
W:	chadhillhotel.co.uk
Bedrooms:	14 • £48.00-£58.00 per double room per night, breakfast included
Open:	Seasonal opening – call for details
Description:	Enjoy this charming, Victorian mansion with a relaxed atmosphere set in a quiet, central area of Sandown with private parking. Close to all amenities.
Facilities:	
To Beach:	0.25 miles

SANDOWN

Denewood Hotel ♦♦♦♦Guest Accommodation

7-9 Victoria Road, Sandown, Isle of Wight, PO36 8AL

T:	+44 (0) 1983 402980
E:	holidays@denewoodhotel.co.uk
W:	denewood-hotel.co.uk
Bedrooms:	14 • £54.00-£70.00 per double room per night, breakfast included • Debit/credit card accepted
Open:	Seasonal opening – call for details
Description:	Denewood is the perfect location from which to explore this historic and beautiful island, or to relax on Sandown's famous golden sands – just two minutes away. Guests are given a warm welcome in comfortable and friendly surroundings.
Facilities:	
To Beach:	0.17 miles

SANDOWN

Melville Hall Hotel & Utopia Spa ★★★Hotel

Melville Street, Sandown, Isle of Wight, PO36 9DH

T:	+44 (0) 1983 400500
E:	enquiries@melvillehall.co.uk
W:	melvillehall.co.uk
Bedrooms:	30 • £90.00 per double room per night, breakfast included • Debit/credit card accepted
Open:	Seasonal opening – call for details
Description:	Melville Hall has undergone extensive refurbishment to ensure visitors have a comfortable and relaxing stay. It is only a few minutes' stroll from the seafront, cliff walk and shops.
Facilities:	
To Beach:	0.27 miles

SANDOWN

Montrene Hotel ★★Hotel

Avenue Road, Sandown, Isle of Wight, PO36 8BN

T:	+44 (0) 1983 403722
E:	enquiries@montrene.co.uk
W:	montrene.co.uk
Bedrooms:	41 • £74.00-£92.00 per double room per night, breakfast included • Debit/credit card accepted
Open:	Seasonal opening – call for details
Description:	Situated in secluded grounds, yet only moments from Sandown's famous beach, Montrene offers the best for a perfect holiday or Christmas/New Year break.
Facilities:	P
To Beach:	0.33 miles

SANDOWN

Ocean Hotel ★★Hotel

Esplanade, Sandown, Isle of Wight, PO36 8AB

T:	+44 (0) 1983 402351
E:	oceanhotel@aol.com
W:	ocean-hotel.co.uk
Bedrooms:	96 • £78.00 per double room per night, breakfast included • Debit/credit card accepted
Open:	Seasonal opening – call for details
Description:	The Ocean Hotel, set in large attractive gardens, is conveniently placed in the High Street. The Esplanade with the long, sandy and safe beach of Sandown Bay is only a few steps away.
Facilities:	P
To Beach:	0.07 miles

SANDOWN

The Winchester Park Hotel ★★Guesthouse

Fitzroy Street, Sandown, Isle of Wight, PO36 8HQ

T:	+44 (0) 1983 402619
E:	reception@winchesterparkhotel.co.uk
W:	winchesterparkhotel.co.uk
Bedrooms:	17 • £50.00-£54.00 per double room per night, breakfast included • Debit/credit card accepted
Open:	Seasonal opening – call for details
Description:	The Winchester Park Hotel is a family hotel conveniently situated within a few minutes' walk of the centre of Sandown and the seafront, and close to both the island's airports.
Facilities:	P
To Beach:	0.18 miles

SHANKLIN

Bay House Hotel ★★Hotel

8 Chine Avenue, Keats Green, Shanklin, Isle of Wight, PO37 6AG

T:	+44 (0) 1983 863180
E:	bayhousehotel@zoom.co.uk
W:	bayhouse-hotel.co.uk
Bedrooms:	21 • £54.00 per double room per night, breakfast included • Debit/credit card accepted
Open:	Seasonal opening – call for details
Description:	In a fine position overlooking the Bay on Keats Green with uninterrupted sea views. Located in a quiet position away from the main road, yet five minutes' walk from the beach.
Facilities:	
To Beach:	0.5 miles

SHANKLIN

Chestnut Mews Holiday Cottages★★★★★Self Catering

14 Vaughan Way, Old Village, Shanklin, Isle of Wight, PO37 6SD

T:	+44 (0) 1983 869000
E:	chestnutmews@btinternet.com
W:	chestnutmews.co.uk
Units:	4 • £250.00-£900.00 per unit per week
Open:	Seasonal opening – call for details
Description:	A true haven of tranquillity and relaxation awaits you. Nestled in a beautiful, sylvan setting with 0.5 acres of sheltered, secluded gardens. The four, newly-built, self-catering cottages offer luxurious accommodation.
Facilities:	
To Beach:	0.94 miles

SHANKLIN

Clifton Hotel ★★Hotel

Keats Green, 1 Queens Road, Shanklin, Isle of Wight, PO37 6AN

T:	+44 (0) 1983 863015
E:	grahamsitton@hotmail.com
W:	hotelclifton.co.uk
Bedrooms:	17 • £96.00 per double room per night, breakfast included • Debit/credit card accepted
Open:	Year round
Description:	The Clifton is a family-run hotel standing in its own grounds in a peaceful, traffic-free location leading onto Keats Green, one of the island's most beautiful cliff top walks.
Facilities:	
To Beach:	0.39 miles

SHANKLIN

Edgecliffe Hotel ♦♦♦♦Guest Accommodation

7 Clarence Gardens, Shanklin, Isle of Wight, PO37 6HA

T: +44 (0) 1983 866199
E: edgecliffehtl@aol.com
W: wightonline.co.uk/edgecliffehotel

Bedrooms: 10 • £48.00-£64.00 per double room per night, breakfast included • Debit/credit card accepted

Open: Seasonal opening – call for details

Description: Built in the early 1900s, the Victorian-style Edgecliffe Hotel provides the ideal holiday retreat. All guest rooms, from singles to four-poster, are comfortable and tastefully decorated.

Facilities:

To Beach: 0.13 miles

SHANKLIN

Fernbank Hotel ★★Hotel

Highfield Road, Shanklin, Isle of Wight, PO37 6PP

T: +44 (0) 1983 862790
E: fernbankhotel@tiscali.co.uk
W: fernbankhotel.net

Bedrooms: 19 • £64.00-£110.00 per double room per night, breakfast included • Debit/credit card accepted

Open: Year round

Description: Are you looking for somewhere special? Then look no further than the Fernbank, the 'Jewel of the Isle of Wight', which is located adjacent to the Old Village, yet only minutes from the downs and beach.

Facilities:

To Beach: 0.71 miles

SHANKLIN

Grange Bank House ♦♦♦♦Guest Accommodation

Grange Road, Shanklin, Isle of Wight, PO37 6NN SILVER AWARD

T: +44 (0) 1983 862337
E: grangebank@btinternet.com
W: grangebank.co.uk

Bedrooms: 10 • £52.00-£62.00 per double room per night, breakfast included • Debit/credit card accepted

Open: Seasonal opening – call for details

Description: Grange Bank is a friendly, non-smoking premises run by members of one family since 1972. Ideally situated in the picturesque Old Village, it is just a short stroll from Rylstone Gardens, the Big Mead, Chine, beach, shops and theatre.

Facilities:

To Beach: 0.66 miles

SHANKLIN

Havelock Hotel ♦♦♦♦Guest Accommodation

2 Queens Road, Shanklin, Isle of Wight, PO37 6AN GOLD AWARD

T:	+44 (0) 1983 862747
E:	enquiries@havelockhotel.co.uk
W:	havelockhotel.co.uk
Bedrooms:	22 • £54.00-£70.00 per double room per night, breakfast included • Debit/credit card accepted
Open:	Seasonal opening – call for details
Description:	Set in mature gardens, this unique B&B hotel, offers excellent facilities, value and personal service.
Facilities:	P
To Beach:	0.39 miles

SHANKLIN

Landguard Camping Park ★★★★Camping & Touring Park

Landguard Manor Road, Shanklin, Isle of Wight, PO37 7PH

T:	+44 (0) 1983 867028
E:	landguard@weltinet.com
W:	landguard-camping.co.uk
Pitches:	150 • £11.50-£15.00 per caravan per night • Debit/credit card accepted
Open:	Seasonal opening – call for details
Description:	This family park offers quality camping for all touring units. Surrounded by trees in a rural setting, the park is just 10 minutes' stroll to Shanklin town centre. Within one mile are the sandy beaches of Sandown Bay.
Facilities:	
To Beach:	0.5 miles

SHANKLIN

Lower Hyde Holiday Village

★★★★Holiday, Touring & Camping Park

Landguard Road, Shanklin, Isle of Wight, PO37 7LL ROSE AWARD

T:	+44 (0) 871 664 9751
E:	holidaysales.lowerhyde@park-resorts.com
W:	park-resorts.com
Pitches:	305 • £17.00 per motor caravan per night
Open:	Seasonal opening – call for details
Description:	Lower Hyde, on the outskirts of Shanklin, is close to the sandy, sunshine beaches of the south-east of the island and the fun-packed attractions for all the family.
Facilities:	
To Beach:	0.5 miles

SHANKLIN

Luccombe Hall Country House Hotel ★★★Hotel

8 Luccombe Road, Shanklin, Isle of Wight, PO37 6RL

T: +44 (0) 1983 869000
E: reservations@luccombehall.co.uk
W: luccombehall.co.uk

Bedrooms: 30 • £70.00 per double room per night, breakfast included • Debit/credit card accepted

Open: Seasonal opening – call for details

Description: Built in 1870 as the Summer Palace for the Bishop of Portsmouth this lovely, family-run hotel commands magnificent views of the bay with direct access to the beach and the Old Village of Shanklin, yet is away from traffic.

Facilities: P

To Beach: 0.73 miles

SHANKLIN

Luccombe Villa ★★★Self Catering

9 Popham Road, Shanklin, Isle of Wight, PO37 6RF

T: +44 (0) 1983 869000
E: info@luccombevilla.co.uk
W: luccombevilla.co.uk

Units: 7 • £150.00-£660.00 per unit per week

Open: Seasonal opening – call for details

Description: Luccombe Villa is an elegant, stone-built, Victorian house standing in secluded gardens, and in a marvellous position between Shanklin Old Village and the sea. Easy walk to Shanklin Chine, Rylstone Gardens and the sandy beach.

Facilities: P

To Beach: 0.8 miles

SHANKLIN

Lyon Court ★★★Self Catering

Westhill Road, Shanklin, Isle of Wight, PO37 6PZ

T: +44 (0) 1983 869000
E: info@lyoncourtshanklin.co.uk
W: lyoncourtshanklin.co.uk

Units: 8 • £190.00-£710.00 per unit per week

Open: Seasonal opening – call for details

Description: Lyon Court is an elegant country house in an idyllic setting, just a 10-minute walk from Shanklin Old Village and town centre. Tastefully converted to provide eight individual, quality apartments.

Facilities: P

To Beach: 0.86 miles

SHANKLIN

Roseglen Hotel ♦♦♦♦Guest Accommodation

12 Palmerston Road, Shanklin, Isle of Wight, PO37 6AS

T: +44 (0) 1983 863164
E: angela@roseglen.co.uk
W: roseglen.co.uk

Bedrooms: 14 • £52.00 per double room per night, breakfast included • Debit/credit card accepted

Open: Seasonal opening – call for details

Description: The Roseglen is the perfect venue to spend summer holidays or short breaks. It's a family-run, friendly hotel.

Facilities:

To Beach: 0.37 miles

SHANKLIN

Roseberry Hotel ★★Hotel

3 Alexandra Road, Shanklin, Isle of Wight, PO37 6AF

T: +44 (0) 1983 862805
E: herm-beach@tinyworld.co.uk
W: roseberryhotel-isleofwight.co.uk

Bedrooms: 18 • £62.00 per double room per night, breakfast included • Debit/credit card accepted

Open: Year round

Description: The Roseberry occupies one of the finest positions in Shanklin, standing in its own beautiful garden. A family-run hotel with TV lounge, bar, restaurant, sun lounge/toy room with Playstation.

Facilities:

To Beach: 0.43 miles

SHANKLIN

Rylstone Manor Hotel ★★★Country House Hotel

Rylstone Gardens, Popham Road, Shanklin, Isle of Wight, PO37 6RG

T: +44 (0) 1983 862806
E: rylstonemanor@btinternet.com
W: rylstone-manor.co.uk

Bedrooms: 9 • £100.00 per double room per night, breakfast included • Debit/credit card accepted

Open: Year round

Description: This lovely Grade II Listed manor house , a country house with style, sits amid four acres of the beautiful Rylstone Gardens and commands views over the famous Shanklin Chine and the sea beyond.

Facilities:

To Beach: 0.7 miles

SHANKLIN

Snowdon Hotel

★★★★Guest Accommodation

19 Queens Road, Shanklin, Isle of Wight, PO37 6AW

SILVER AWARD

T:	+44 (0) 1983 862853
E:	info@snowdonhotel.fsnet.co.uk
W:	thesnowdonhotel.co.uk
Bedrooms:	8 • £52.00-£56.00 per double room per night, breakfast included • Debit/credit card accepted
Open:	Seasonal opening – call for details
Description:	The Snowdon Hotel is a non-smoking, family-run hotel just 100 metres away from the spectacular cliff walk and views of Sandown Bay.
Facilities:	[facility symbols]
To Beach:	0.3 miles

SHANKLIN

Summerhill Apartments

★★★★Self Catering

4 Culver Road, Shanklin, Isle of Wight, PO37 6ER

T:	+44 (0) 1983 868898
E:	jean@summerhillapts.co.uk
W:	summerhillapts.co.uk
Units:	8 • £240.00-£765.00 per unit per week • Debit/credit card accepted
Open:	Seasonal opening – call for details
Description:	Spacious and comfortable, self-contained apartment in a Victorian gentleman's residence, a short walk away from the Old Village.
Facilities:	[facility symbols]
To Beach:	0.11 miles

SHANKLIN

The Fawley Guesthouse

★★★★Guesthouse

12 Hope Road, Shanklin, Isle of Wight, PO37 6EA

T:	+44 (0) 1983 868898
E:	enquiries@the-fawley.co.uk
W:	the-fawley.co.uk
Bedrooms:	10 • £52.00-£60.00 per double room per night, breakfast included • Debit/credit card accepted
Open:	Seasonal opening – call for details
Description:	The Fawley is a friendly, family-run hotel, just five minutes' walk from the safe, sandy beach. It is also a short stroll to the station, town centre and the Old Village.
Facilities:	[facility symbols]
To Beach:	0.1 miles

SHANKLIN

Upper Chine Holiday Cottages & Apartments

★★★★Self Catering

22A Church Road, Shanklin, Isle of Wight, PO37 6QR

T:	+44 (0) 1983 869000
E:	upperchine@btconnect.com
W:	upperchinecottages.co.uk
Units:	16 • £200.00-£800.00 per unit per week • Debit/credit card accepted
Open:	Seasonal opening – call for details
Description:	Enjoy a luxury, self-catering holiday in the Old Village of Shanklin in one of our 10 individually designed cottages or six spacious, modern apartments, all beautifully equipped to a very high standard with a patio or balcony.
Facilities:	
To Beach:	0.87 miles

SHANKLIN

Willow Bank Hotel

★★★Guesthouse

36 Atherley Road, Shanklin, Isle of Wight, PO37 7AU

T:	+44 (0) 1983 862482
E:	info@willowbankhotel.co.uk
W:	willowbankhotel.co.uk
Bedrooms:	7 • £50.00 per double room per night, breakfast included • Debit/credit card accepted
Open:	Seasonal opening – call for details
Description:	Home-from-home, family-run hotel, close to all amenities, shops, safe beaches and railway. Pets, families and one nighters very welcome.
Facilities:	
To Beach:	0.2 miles

SHANKLIN

YMCA Winchester House

★★★Self Catering

Sandown Road, Shanklin, Isle of Wight, PO37 6HU

T:	+44 (0) 1983 862805
E:	info@ymca-fg.org
W:	winchesterhouse.org.uk
Units:	2 • £308.00-£2,100.00 per unit per week
Open:	Seasonal opening – call for details
Description:	Winchester House is a beautiful, Victorian building set in large grounds on the cliff top overlooking Sandown Bay and immediately above the long, sandy beach.
Facilities:	
To Beach:	0.45 miles

TOTLAND BAY

Country Garden Hotel ♦♦♦♦Guest Accommodation

Church Hill, Totland Bay, Isle of Wight, PO39 0ET SILVER AWARD

T: +44 (0) 1983 754521
E: countrygardeniow@aol.com
W: thecountrygardenhotel.co.uk

Bedrooms: 16 • £90.00-£155.00 per double room per night, breakfast included • Debit/credit card accepted

Open: Seasonal opening – call for details

Description: Our delightful, adults-only, intimate hotel in tranquil West Wight is set in lovely gardens that are a riot of colour most of the year. It is a five-minute stroll to the Solent; easy access to lovely walks including Tennyson Down and the Needles.

Facilities:

To Beach: 0.79 miles

TOTLAND BAY

Sandy Lane B&B ★★★★Guesthouse

Sandy Lane, Colwell Common Road, Totland Bay, Isle of Wight, PO39 0DD

T: +44 (0) 1983 752240
E: louise@sandylane-iow.co.uk
W: sandylane-iow.co.uk

Bedrooms: 5 • £48.00-£58.00 per double room per night, breakfast included

Open: Year round except Christmas and New Year

Description: Relaxed, family-run B&B. Bedrooms comfortably furnished. Four minutes' walk to beautiful Colwell Bay with picturesque surrounding countryside.

Facilities:

To Beach: 0.28 miles

TOTLAND BAY

Sentry Mead Hotel ★★★Hotel

Madeira Road, Totland Bay, Isle of Wight, PO39 0BJ SILVER AWARD

T: +44 (0) 1983 753212
E: info@sentrymead.co.uk
W: sentrymead.co.uk

Bedrooms: 14 • £90.00-£120.00 per double room per night, breakfast included • Debit/credit card accepted

Open: Seasonal opening – call for details

Description: Sentry Mead Hotel is a beautiful Victorian country house set in its own spacious gardens in the tranquil surroundings of West Wight.

Facilities:

To Beach: 0.46 miles

VENTNOR

Bonchurch Manor ♦♦♦♦Guest Accommodation

Bonchurch Shute, Bonchurch, Ventnor, Isle of Wight, PO38 1NU

T:	+44 (0) 1983 852868
E:	reception@bonchurchmanor.com
W:	bonchurchmanor.com
Bedrooms:	14 • £90.00-£110.00 per double room per night, breakfast included • Debit/credit card accepted
Open:	Seasonal opening – call for details
Description:	Bonchurch Manor is an early 19thC Victorian country house set in a quiet village. The two-acre garden within the hotel backs on to the cliffs with its own cave. Stunning views across the sea.
Facilities:	
To Beach:	0.85 miles

VENTNOR

Burlington Hotel (Ventnor) ★★★Hotel

Bellevue Road, Ventnor, Isle of Wight, PO38 1DB

T:	+44 (0) 1983 852113
E:	mctoldridge@burlingtonhotel.freeserve.co.uk
W:	burlingtonhotel.uk.com
Bedrooms:	24 • £68.00 per double room per night, breakfast included • Debit/credit card accepted
Open:	Seasonal opening – call for details
Description:	The Burlington is one of the island's top graded hotels and has been run by the McToldridge family for more than 35 years, offering first class accommodation and friendly service in a relaxed and peaceful atmosphere.
Facilities:	
To Beach:	0.36 miles

VENTNOR

Lake Hotel ★★★★Guest Accommodation

Shore Road, Bonchurch, Ventnor, Isle of Wight, PO38 1RF

T:	+44 (0) 1983 852613
E:	enquiries@lakehotel.co.uk
W:	lakehotel.co.uk
Bedrooms:	20 • £68.00-£78.00 per double room per night, breakfast included
Open:	Seasonal opening – call for details
Description:	This lovely, country house hotel is set in a beautiful quiet two acre garden on the seaward side of the olde worlde village of Bonchurch.
Facilities:	
To Beach:	0.62 miles

VENTNOR

St Maur Hotel

★★Hotel

Castle Road, Ventnor, Isle of Wight, PO38 1LG

SILVER AWARD

T:	+44 (0) 1983 852570
E:	sales@stmaur.co.uk
W:	stmaur.co.uk
Bedrooms:	11 • £68.00-£112.00 per double room per night, breakfast included • Debit/credit card accepted
Open:	Seasonal opening – call for details
Description:	Owned by the same family since 1966, the hotel has built a reputation for good, home-cooked food and friendly service.
Facilities:	
To Beach:	0.64 miles

VENTNOR

The Leconfield

♦♦♦♦Guest Accommodation

85 Leeson Road, Upper Bonchurch, Ventnor, PO38 1PU

SILVER AWARD

T:	+44 (0) 1983 852196
E:	enquiries@leconfieldhotel.com
W:	leconfieldhotel.com
Bedrooms:	13 • £74.00-£162.00 per double room per night, breakfast included • Debit/credit card accepted
Open:	Seasonal opening – call for details
Description:	The Leconfield is set into Bonchurch Downs on the pretty southern side of the Isle of Wight. The owners welcome you to their Victorian country home with spectacular, panoramic sea views.
Facilities:	
To Beach:	1.02 miles

WROXALL – VENTNOR BEACH

Little Span Farm B&B

★★★Farm

Rew Lane, Wroxall, Ventnor, Isle of Wight, PO38 3AU

T:	+44 (0) 1983 852419
E:	info@spanfarm.co.uk
W:	spanfarm.co.uk
Bedrooms:	4 • £44.00-£50.00 per double room per night, breakfast included
Open:	Seasonal opening – call for details
Description:	Arable/sheep farm in Area of Outstanding Natural Beauty. Beach and golf course approximately two miles.
Facilities:	
To Beach:	1.7 miles

BIRCHINGTON – WEST BAY, WESTGATE

Quex Caravan Park ★★★★★Holiday & Touring Park

Park Road, Birchington, Kent, CT7 0BL

T:	+44 (0) 1843 841273
E:	info@keatfarm.co.uk
W:	keatfarm.co.uk
Pitches:	50 • £13.50-£16.00 per caravan per night • Debit/credit card accepted
Open:	Seasonal opening – call for details
Description:	Flat, grassy park amid farmland, only a short distance from Ramsgate and Margate. Channel ports within easy reach.
Facilities:	P
To Beach:	1.06 miles

BIRCHINGTON – WEST BAY, WESTGATE

Two Chimneys Holiday Park

★★★★★Holiday, Touring & Camping Park

Shottendane Road, Birchington, Kent, CT7 0HD

T:	+44 (0) 1843 841068
E:	info@twochimneys.co.uk
W:	twochimneys.co.uk
Pitches:	202 • £11.00-£18.00 per caravan per night • Debit/credit card; cheques/cash accepted
Open:	Seasonal opening – call for details
Description:	A lovely, country site close to main holiday attractions, sandy beaches and Channel ports. Canterbury 13 miles. Scenic Kent countryside.
Facilities:	P
To Beach:	1.24 miles

BROADSTAIRS – VIKING BAY

Pierremont ♦♦♦Guest Accommodation

102 Pierremont Avenue, Broadstairs, Kent, CT10 1NT

T:	+44 (0) 1843 600462
E:	peter@pierremontguesthouse.co.uk
W:	pierremontguesthouse.co.uk
Bedrooms:	2 • £45.00 per double room per night, breakfast included
Open:	Year round
Description:	Edwardian house near seafront and town. One double and twin room, shared bathroom on first floor. Ideal for four friends/family.
Facilities:	P
To Beach:	0.29 miles

MARGATE – MARGATE, MAIN SANDS

YHA Margate The Beachcomber ★★Hostel

3-4 Royal Esplanade, Westbrook Bay, Margate, Kent, CT9 5DL

T:	+44 (0) 1843 221616
E:	margate@yha.org.uk
W:	yha.org.uk
Bedrooms:	15 • £9.00-£12.50 per person per night, room only • Debit/credit card; cheques/cash accepted
Open:	Year round except Christmas and New Year
Description:	Converted hotel next to sandy beach. Offers clean, simple, budget accommodation to cyclists, walkers, families and youth/school/church/family groups.
Facilities:	
To Beach:	0.5 miles

RAMSGATE – RAMSGATE MAIN SANDS

Spencer Court Hotel ♦♦♦Guest Accommodation

37 Spencer Square, Ramsgate, Kent, CT11 9LD

T:	+44 (0) 1843 594582
E:	glendaandken@hotmail.com
W:	smoothhound.co.uk/hotels/spencer.ltml
Bedrooms:	9 • £50.00-£60.00 per double room per night, breakfast included • Cheques/cash accepted
Open:	Year round
Description:	Grade II Listed building in quiet square with garden overlooking tennis courts. Three hundred metres from seafront, directly above ferry terminals.
Facilities:	
To Beach:	0.47 miles

WARDEN – LEYSDOWN BEACH

Warden Springs Holiday Park ★★★★Holiday, Touring & Camping Park

Thorn Hill Road, Eastchurch, Sheerness, Kent, ME12 4HF

T:	+44 (0) 871 664 9790
E:	holidayparks.wardensprings@park-resorts.com
W:	park-resorts.com
Pitches:	119 • £9.50-£14.50 per caravan per night • Debit/credit card accepted
Open:	Seasonal opening – call for details
Description:	Secluded, woodland setting that overlooks bay. Own shop, clubhouse, laundry, showers and toilets, and heated pool. Adjoining barbecue and bar in clubhouse. Nine-hole pitch and putt.
Facilities:	
To Beach:	1.68 miles

WESTGATE-ON-SEA – WEST BAY

White Lodge Guesthouse ♦♦♦Guest Accommodation

12 Domneva Road, Westgate-on-Sea, Kent, CT8 8PE

T:	+44 (0) 1843 831828
E:	whitelodge.thanet@btinternet.com
W:	whitelodge.thanet.btinternet.co.uk
Bedrooms:	6 • £45.00-£55.00 per double room per night, breakfast included • Debit/credit card accepted
Open:	Year round
Description:	A detached guesthouse in a quiet road 100 yards from Westgate's sandy bay. Five minutes from town/railway station.
Facilities:	
To Beach:	0.1 miles

WHITSTABLE – TANKERTON BEACH

Copeland House ♦♦♦Guest Accommodation

4 Island Wall, Whitstable, Kent, CT5 1EP

T:	+44 (0) 1227 266207
E:	mail@copelandhouse.co.uk
W:	copelandhouse.co.uk
Bedrooms:	4 • £50.00-£90.00 per double room per night, breakfast included
Open:	Year round except Christmas
Description:	Close to beach, 100 yards from town centre and famous seafood restaurants, yet in quiet location. Stylish, comfortable, en suite rooms.
Facilities:	
To Beach:	1.22 miles

WHITSTABLE – TANKERTON BEACH

The Duke of Cumberland ♦♦♦Guest Accommodation

High Street, Whitstable, Kent, CT5 1AP

T:	+44 (0) 1227 280617
E:	enquiries@thedukeinwhitstable.co.uk
W:	thedukeinwhitstable.co.uk
Bedrooms:	8 • £60.00-£170.00 per double room per night, breakfast included • Debit/credit card accepted
Open:	Year round
Description:	Central location for beach, harbour and shopping. The restaurant serves dishes made from locally-sourced produce. Bedrooms refurbished in 2004. Functions catered for.
Facilities:	
To Beach:	1.2 miles

WHITSTABLE – TANKERTON BEACH

The Marine Hotel ★★Hotel

Marine Parade, Whitstable, Kent, CT5 2BE

T: +44 (0) 1227 272672
E: marine@shepherd-neame.co.uk
W: shepherd-neame.co.uk

Bedrooms: 31 • £75.00 per double room per night, breakfast included • Debit/credit card; cheques/cash accepted

Open: Year round

Description: Traditional hotel, 31 en suite bedrooms, 20 sea-facing rooms and 10 of those with balconies. Shepherd Neame ales. Daily menu with fresh local produce.

Facilities:

To Beach: 0.24 miles

WHITSTABLE – TANKERTON BEACH

The Pearl Fisher ♦♦♦♦Guest Accommodation

103 Cromwell Road, Whitstable, Kent, CT5 1NL SILVER AWARD

T: +44 (0) 1227 771000
E: stay@thepearlfisher.co.uk
W: thepearlfisher.com

Bedrooms: 3 • £60.00-£95.00 per double room per night, breakfast included • Debit/credit card accepted

Open: Year round

Description: Ideally located in Whitstable's conservation area, a short stroll from the harbour, seafront, town centre and railway station.

Facilities: P

To Beach: 1.04 miles

BLACKPOOL – BOULEVARD BEACH

Beachcliffe Holiday Flats ★★★Self Catering

3 King Edward Avenue, Blackpool, Lancashire, FY2 9TD

T: +44 (0) 1253 357147
E: stay@beachcliffe.com
W: beachcliffe.com

Units: 5 • £160.00-£350.00 per unit per week

Open: Year round

Description: The Beachcliffe Holiday Flats are fully self-contained, well decorated, furnished and equipped to a high standard, all with full central heating.

Facilities: P TV

To Beach: 0.8 miles

BLACKPOOL – BOULEVARD BEACH

Berwick Hotel ♦♦♦♦Guest Accommodation

23 King Edward Avenue, Blackpool, Lancashire, FY2 9TA

T:	+44 (0) 1253 351496
E:	theberwickhotel@btconnect.com
W:	theberwickhotel.co.uk
Bedrooms:	8 • £42.00-£58.00 per double room per night, breakfast included • Debit/credit card accepted
Open:	Year round except New Year
Description:	This small, friendly hotel is ideally situated in North Shore, adjacent to Queens Promenade and close to Gynn Gardens.
Facilities:	
To Beach:	0.81 miles

BLACKPOOL – BOULEVARD BEACH

Berwyn Hotel ★★★Guest Accommodation

1-2 Finchley Road, Blackpool, Lancashire, FY1 2LP

T:	+44 (0) 1253 352896
E:	stay@berwynhotel.co.uk
W:	berwynhotel.co.uk
Bedrooms:	20 • £45.00-£90.00 per double room per night, breakfast included • Debit/credit card accepted
Open:	Year round except Christmas and New Year
Description:	The Berwyn is pleasantly situated overlooking the attractive Gynn Gardens and the sea beyond. The standards of cuisine, service and cleanliness are high, and the aim is to please.
Facilities:	
To Beach:	0.6 miles

BLACKPOOL – BOULEVARD BEACH

Braeside Hotel ★★Guest Accommodation

6 Willshaw Road, Blackpool, Lancashire, FY2 9SH

T:	+44 (0) 1253 351363
E:	enq@thebraeside.co.uk
W:	thebraeside.co.uk
Bedrooms:	8 • £38.00-£48.00 per double room per night, breakfast included • Debit/credit card accepted
Open:	Year round except Christmas
Description:	Friendly, family-run guesthouse overlooking Gynn Gardens in the North Shore area. Close to the attractions but in a quieter location.
Facilities:	
To Beach:	0.69 miles

BLACKPOOL – BOULEVARD BEACH

Brooklands Hotel ♦♦♦Guest Accommodation

28-30 King Edward Avenue, Blackpool, Lancashire, FY2 9TA

T:	+44 (0) 1253 351479
E:	brooklandhotel@btinternet.com
W:	brooklands-hotel.com
Bedrooms:	18 • £44.00-£56.00 per double room per night, breakfast included • Debit/credit card accepted
Open:	Year round except Christmas and New Year
Description:	The Brooklands is in the most select part of Blackpool. It is renowned for the quality of its traditional, home-cooked meals and all the friendliness associated with a family-run hotel.
Facilities:	
To Beach:	0.81 miles

BLACKPOOL – BOULEVARD BEACH

Denely Private Hotel ♦♦♦Guest Accommodation

15 King Edward Avenue, Blackpool, Lancashire, FY2 9TA

T:	+44 (0) 1253 352757
E:	denely@tesco.net
W:	denelyhotel.co.uk
Bedrooms:	18 • £37.00-£45.00 per double room per night, breakfast included • Debit/credit card accepted
Open:	Seasonal opening – call for details
Description:	Small, family establishment that enjoys a good location and offers a good standard of comfortable accommodation that benefits from a good standard of customer care and service.
Facilities:	
To Beach:	0.81 miles

BLACKPOOL – BOULEVARD BEACH

Ellan Vannin ★★★Guest Accommodation

6 Gynn Avenue, Blackpool, Lancashire, FY1 2LD

T:	+44 (0) 1253 351784
E:	the_ellan_vannin@hotmail.com
W:	the-ellan-vannin.co.uk
Bedrooms:	7 • £40.00-£60.00 per double room per night, breakfast included • Debit/credit card accepted
Open:	Seasonal opening – call for details
Description:	A warm welcome awaits you at the small and friendly Ellan Vannin guesthouse where the owners strive to achieve a high standard of food and cleanliness.
Facilities:	
To Beach:	0.5 miles

BLACKPOOL – BOULEVARD BEACH

Liberty's Hotel on the Square ★★Hotel

Cocker Square, Blackpool, Lancashire, FY1 1RX

T: +44 (0) 1253 291155
E: gm.bla@washearings.com
W: thealabama.co.uk

Bedrooms: 68 • £60.00-£90.00 per double room per night, breakfast included • Debit/credit card accepted

Open: Year round except Christmas and New Year

Description: Situated on the Promenade, close to the centre of Blackpool. Liberty's offers a live entertainment venue and a Health and Leisure Club.

Facilities: [symbols]

To Beach: 0.11 miles

BLACKPOOL – BOULEVARD BEACH

Manor Private Hotel ★★★Guest Accommodation

32 Queens Promenade, Blackpool, Lancashire, FY2 9RN

T: +44 (0) 1253 351446
E: accommodation@blackpool-hotels-manor.co.uk
W: blackpool-hotels-manor.co.uk

Bedrooms: 28 • £20.00-£40.00 per double room per night, breakfast included • Debit/credit card accepted

Open: Year round

Description: Fabulous, seafront hotel on the refined North Shore Queens Promenade. Discounts available for seniors and children all year round. Traditional Turkey & Tinsel breaks and full board. Great entertainments and Christmas and New Year opening.

Facilities: [symbols]

To Beach: 0.87 miles

BLACKPOOL – BOULEVARD BEACH

Oban House Hotel ★★★Guest Accommodation

63 Holmfield Road, Blackpool, Lancashire, FY2 9RU

T: +44 (0) 1253 352413
E: obanhousehotel@aol.com
W: obanhousehotel.co.uk

Bedrooms: 12 • £46.00 per double room per night, breakfast included • Debit/credit card accepted

Open: Seasonal opening – call for details

Description: This is a family-run hotel with a chair lift to the first floor. All home-cooked food; special diets catered for. Child-friendly and it has entertainment in the bar some evenings.

Facilities: [symbols]

To Beach: 0.63 miles

BLACKPOOL – BOULEVARD BEACH

Pembroke Hotel ♦♦♦♦Guest Accommodation

11 King Edward Avenue, Blackpool, Lancashire, FY2 9TD

T:	+44 (0) 1253 351306
E:	info@neartheprom.com
W:	neartheprom.com
Bedrooms:	9 • £42.00-£54.00 per double room per night, breakfast included • Debit/credit card; cheques/cash accepted
Open:	Year round
Description:	The Pembroke is one of the finest small hotels in Blackpool, providing quality, en suite accommodation.
Facilities:	[illegible]
To Beach:	0.8 miles

BLACKPOOL – BOULEVARD BEACH

The Holiday Lodge ★★Self Catering

115 Holmfield Road, Blackpool, Lancashire, FY2 9RF

T:	+44 (0) 1253 351446
E:	mail@holidaylodge.info
W:	holidaylodge.info
Units:	5 • £61.00-£291.00 per unit per week • Debit/credit card; cheques/cash accepted
Open:	Year round
Description:	The Holiday Lodge consists of five, modern, self-contained holiday flats, all en suite, fully equipped for a self-catering holiday, centrally heated with double glazing and situated on the more genteel North Shore.
Facilities:	P
To Beach:	0.98 miles

BLACKPOOL – BOULEVARD BEACH

The Westcliffe ♦♦♦Guest Accommodation

46 King Edward Avenue, Blackpool, Lancashire, FY2 9TA

T:	+44 (0) 1253 352943
E:	westcliffehotel@aol.com
W:	westcliffehotel.com
Bedrooms:	7 • £40.00-£52.00 per double room per night, breakfast included • Debit/credit card accepted
Open:	Year round except Christmas and New Year
Description:	A family-run, non-smoking hotel, small and friendly in this select area, adjacent to Queens Promenade.
Facilities:	P
To Beach:	0.75 miles

BLACKPOOL – CENTRAL BEACH

Aberford Hotel ♦♦♦Guest Accommodation

12-14 Yorkshire Street, Blackpool, Lancashire, FY1 5BG

T:	+44 (0) 1253 625026
E:	info@aberfordhotel.co.uk
W:	aberfordhotel.co.uk
Bedrooms:	21 • £40.00 per double room per night, breakfast included • Debit/credit card accepted
Open:	Year round except Christmas and New Year
Description:	Minutes from Central Pier and the Promenade, the Aberford is an attractive, family-run Victorian hotel that is ideally positioned for all of Blackpool's attractions.
Facilities:	
To Beach:	0.15 miles

BLACKPOOL – CENTRAL BEACH

Alumhurst Hotel ★★Small Hotel

13-15 Charnley Road, Blackpool, Lancashire, FY1 4PE

T:	+44 (0) 1253 620959
E:	alumhurst@btconnect.com
W:	alumhursthotel.com
Bedrooms:	32 • £52.00-£66.00 per double room per night, breakfast included • Debit/credit card; cheques/cash accepted
Open:	Seasonal opening – call for details
Description:	The Alumhurst is a long-established, family-run seasonal hotel in the town centre, near Tower, Winter Gardens, theatres and promenade. It offers en suite rooms for one-four guests with new colour TVs and tea-/coffee-making facilities.
Facilities:	P TV
To Beach:	0.4 miles

BLACKPOOL – CENTRAL BEACH

Ascot Hotel ♦♦♦Guest Accommodation

7 Alexandra Road, Blackpool, Lancashire, FY1 6BU

T:	+44 (0) 1253 346439
E:	info@ascothotel.co.uk
W:	ascothotel.co.uk
Bedrooms:	13 • £44.00-£70.00 per double room per night, breakfast included • Debit/credit card accepted
Open:	Year round except Christmas and New Year
Description:	The Ascot is ideally situated in the heart of the popular Blackpool South Shore area.
Facilities:	P
To Beach:	0.68 miles

BLACKPOOL – CENTRAL BEACH

Beachwood Hotel ★★★Guest Accommodation

30 Moore Street, Blackpool, Lancashire, FY4 1DA

T:	+44 (0) 1253 401951
E:	m.coles@tesco.net
W:	hwoodhotel.co.uk
Bedrooms:	6 • £32.00-£40.00 per double room per night, breakfast included • Debit/credit card accepted
Open:	Year round
Description:	Small, family-run B&B. All rooms en suite, close to all major amenities.
Facilities:	
To Beach:	0.97 miles

BLACKPOOL – CENTRAL BEACH

Beverley Hotel ★★★Guest Accommodation

25 Dean Street, Blackpool, Lancashire, FY4 1AU

T:	+44 (0) 1253 344426
E:	holiday@beverleyhotel-blackpool.co.uk
W:	beverleyhotel-blackpool.co.uk
Bedrooms:	10 • £19.00-£22.00 per double room per night, breakfast included • Debit/credit card accepted
Open:	Year round except Christmas
Description:	The owners invite you to spend your holiday at the Beverley Hotel, which is ideally situated adjacent to the Promenade, South Pier, Sandcastle Waterworld, Casino complex and the Pleasure Beach.
Facilities:	
To Beach:	1.01 miles

BLACKPOOL – CENTRAL BEACH

Big Blue Hotel ★★★★Hotel

Blackpool Pleasure Beach, Ocean Boulevard, Blackpool, Lancashire, FY4 1ND

T:	+44 (0) 845 367 3333
E:	reservations@bigbluehotel.com
W:	blackpoolpleasurebeach.com
Bedrooms:	92 • £95.00 per double room per night, breakfast included • Debit/credit card accepted
Open:	Year round
Description:	The newest hip and chic hotel in Blackpool offering the latest in luxury holiday or business accommodation.
Facilities:	
To Beach:	1.62 miles

BLACKPOOL – CENTRAL BEACH

Boltonia Hotel ♦♦♦Guest Accommodation

124-126 Albert Road, Blackpool, Lancashire, FY1 4PN

T: +44 (0) 1253 620248
E: info@boltoniahotel.co.uk
W: boltoniahotel.co.uk

Bedrooms: 21 • £46.00-£65.00 per double room per night, breakfast included • Debit/credit card accepted

Open: Year round except Christmas

Description: Hotel with all en suite bedrooms, TV, tea-/coffee-making facilities and hairdryers. Dining room is non-smoking and non-smoking rooms are available. Bar with pool table and fruit machine. On-site parking for 12 cars.

Facilities:

To Beach: 0.49 miles

BLACKPOOL – CENTRAL BEACH

Glenholme Hotel ♦♦♦Guest Accommodation

44 Alexandra Road, Blackpool, Lancashire, FY1 6BU

T: +44 (0) 1253 345823
E: glenholme44@yahoo.co.uk
W: glenholmehotel.co.uk

Bedrooms: 12 • £46.00 per double room per night, breakfast included • Debit/credit card; cheques/cash accepted

Open: Year round

Description: A traditional, Victorian building which has been brought into the 21st century to provide excellent, modern accommodation for visitors to Blackpool.

Facilities:

To Beach: 0.68 miles

BLACKPOOL – CENTRAL BEACH

Hurstmere Hotel ★★★Guest Accommodation

5 Alexandra Road, South Shore, Blackpool, Lancashire, FY1 6BU

T: +44 (0) 1253 345843
E: stay@thehurstmerehotel.com
W: thehurstmerehotel.com

Bedrooms: 13 • £50.00-£50.00 per double room per night, breakfast included • Debit/credit card; cheques/cash accepted

Open: Seasonal opening – call for details

Description: This hotel caters exclusively for couples and families. It does not take bookings for hens/stags or single sex groups, which, the owners believe, is why many guests return year after year.

Facilities:

To Beach: 0.68 miles

BLACKPOOL – CENTRAL BEACH

Karen Annes Guesthouse ★★★Guesthouse

4 Barton Avenue, Blackpool, Lancashire, FY1 6AP

T: +44 (0) 1253 346719
E: karen@karen-annes.freeserve.co.uk
W: karenanneshotel.com

Bedrooms: 13 • £24.00-£29.00 per single room per night, breakfast included • Debit/credit card accepted

Open: Year round except Christmas and New Year

Description: Licensed guesthouse, with all en suite facilities, for *couples and seniors only*. A varied menu for both breakfast and evening meal (optional). A few yards from the Promenade.

Facilities:

To Beach: 0.43 miles

BLACKPOOL – CENTRAL BEACH

Kirkstall Hotel ★★★Guest Accommodation

25 Hull Road, Blackpool, Lancashire, FY1 4QB

T: +44 (0) 1253 623077
E: rooms@kirkstallhotel.co.uk
W: kirkstallhotel.co.uk

Bedrooms: 10 • £40.00-£60.00 per double room per night, breakfast included • Debit/credit card; cheques/cash accepted

Open: Year round except Christmas and New Year

Description: The Kirkstall is a centrally located, comfortable, family-run hotel. Due to the excellent service, good home-cooking, cleanliness, friendly atmosphere and outstanding value for money, it is well recommended.

Facilities: P

To Beach: 0.28 miles

BLACKPOOL – CENTRAL BEACH

Le Papillon Hotel ★★★Guesthouse

68 Palatine Road, Blackpool, Lancashire, FY1 4BY

T: +44 (0) 1253 628023
E: le.papillon@btinternet.com
W: lepapillonhotelblackpool.co.uk

Bedrooms: 5 • £45.00-£60.00 per double room per night, breakfast included • Debit/credit card; cheques/cash accepted

Open: Year round except Christmas and New Year

Description: Le Papillon is a small, well presented, family-run guesthouse, situated in a superb, central location.

Facilities: P

To Beach: 0.45 miles

BLACKPOOL – CENTRAL BEACH

Number One ♦♦♦♦♦Guest Accommodation
1 St Lukes Road, Blackpool, Lancashire, FY4 2EL GOLD AWARD

T:	+44 (0) 1253 343901
E:	info@numberoneblackpool.com
W:	numberoneblackpool.com
Bedrooms:	3 • £120.00-£160.00 per double room per night, breakfast included • Debit/credit card; cheques/cash accepted
Open:	Year round except Christmas and New Year
Description:	Number One is Blackpool's only five-diamond Gold B&B. Winner of the Blackpool Tourism Awards' Best Hotel 1-9 Bedrooms 2005, Lancashire & Blackpool Tourist Board's Best B&B 2006/2007. Number One is the ultimate B&B experience!
Facilities:	
To Beach:	1.66 miles

BLACKPOOL – CENTRAL BEACH

Ruskin Hotel ★★Hotel
55-61 Albert Road, Blackpool, Lancashire, FY1 4PW

T:	+44 (0) 1253 624063
E:	ruskinhotel@aol.com
W:	ruskinhotel.com
Bedrooms:	71 • £50.00-£80.00 per double room per night, breakfast included • Debit/credit card; cheques/cash accepted
Open:	Year round except Christmas and New Year
Description:	Centrally located. All rooms en suite with excellent facilities. Fabulous food and entertainment. Four bars, three dance floors, public Bar 'Rolys' and Bistro.Cabaret throughout the year at weekends and nightly in season.
Facilities:	
To Beach:	0.43 miles

BLACKPOOL – CENTRAL BEACH

Waverley Hotel ★★★Guest Accommodation
95 Reads Avenue, Blackpool, Lancashire, FY1 4DG

T:	+44 (0) 1253 621633
E:	wavehotel@aol.com
W:	thewaverleyhotel.com
Bedrooms:	11 • £44.00-£66.00 per double room per night, breakfast included • Debit/credit card accepted
Open:	Seasonal opening – call for details
Description:	Luxury, licensed hotel in central Blackpool. All rooms en suite with modern decoration and facilities. Canopy and four-poster beds available.
Facilities:	
To Beach:	0.42 miles

BLACKPOOL – CENTRAL BEACH

Westfield Hotel ★★★Guest Accommodation

14 Station Road, Blackpool, Lancashire, FY4 1BE

T:	+44 (0) 1253 342468
E:	info@westfieldhotel.co.uk
W:	westfieldhotel.co.uk
Bedrooms:	11 • £46.00-£58.00 per double room per night, breakfast included • Debit/credit card accepted
Open:	Year round
Description:	Beautiful, family hotel with all rooms fully en suite, central heated, Colour TV, tea-/coffee-/hot chocolate-making facilities plus biscuits.
Facilities:	[icons]
To Beach:	1.08 miles

LYTHAM ST ANNES – ST ANNES PIER

Clifton Park Hotel ♦♦♦♦Guest Accommodation

299-301 Clifton Drive South, St Annes-on-Sea, Lytham St Annes, FY8 1HN

T:	+44 (0) 1253 725801
E:	info@cliftonpark.co.uk
W:	cliftonpark.co.uk
Bedrooms:	46 • £95.00 per double room per night, breakfast included • Debit/credit card; cheques/cash accepted
Open:	Year round
Description:	Just 10 minutes from Blackpool's bustling centre the Clifton Park Hotel is in the popular seaside resort of Lytham St Annes. The hotel boasts excellent facilities and a warm, friendly atmosphere.
Facilities:	[icons]
To Beach:	0.24 miles

LYTHAM ST ANNES – ST ANNES PIER

Dalmeny Hotel ★★★Hotel

19-33 South Promenade, St Annes-on-Sea, Lytham St Annes, FY8 1LX

T:	+44 (0) 1253 712236
E:	reservations@dalmenyhotel.co.uk
W:	dalmenyhotel.co.uk
Bedrooms:	128 • £96.00 per double room per night, breakfast included • Debit/credit card; cheques/cash accepted
Open:	Year round except Christmas
Description:	Modern resort hotel, suitable for both families and couples. Full leisure facilities including indoor pool, fitness centre and beauty salon. Conference facilities for up to 200 delegates.
Facilities:	[icons]
To Beach:	0.17 miles

LYTHAM ST ANNES – ST ANNES PIER

Lindum Hotel ★★Hotel

63-67 South Promenade, St Annes-on-Sea, Lytham St Annes, FY8 1LZ

T:	+44 (0) 1253 721534
E:	info@lindumhotel.co.uk
W:	lindumhotel.co.uk
Bedrooms:	88 • £64.00-£110.00 per double room per night, breakfast included • Debit/credit card; cheques/cash accepted
Open:	Year round
Description:	Family-run, seafront hotel with good reputation for cooking and comfortable accommodation. Close to shops and championship golf courses.
Facilities:	[facility symbols]
To Beach:	0.26 miles

LYTHAM ST ANNES – ST ANNES PIER

St Ives Hotel ★★Hotel

7 South Promenade, St Annes-on-Sea, Lytham St Annes, Lancashire, FY8 1LS

T:	+44 (0) 1253 720011
E:	book@st-ives-hotel.co.uk
W:	st-ives-hotel.co.uk
Bedrooms:	66 • £90.00 per double room per night, breakfast included • Debit/credit card; cheques/cash accepted
Open:	Year round except Christmas and New Year
Description:	Comfortable bedrooms all with en suite facilities, satellite TV, telephone, tea-/coffee-making facilities and baby listening. The hotel also has a sauna, hair studio, beauty room, self-service buffet restaurant, pool bar/bar snacks, outdoor/indoor play area and indoor, heated pool.
Facilities:	[facility symbols]
To Beach:	0.1 miles

LYTHAM ST ANNES – ST ANNES PIER

The Chadwick Hotel ★★★Hotel

South Promenade, Lytham St Annes, Lancashire, FY8 1NP

T:	+44 (0) 1253 720061
E:	sales@thechadwickhotel.com
W:	thechadwickhotel.com
Bedrooms:	75 • £66.00 per double room per night, breakfast included • Debit/credit card; cheques/cash accepted
Open:	Year round
Description:	Modern, family-run hotel and leisure complex. Accent on good food, comfort and personal service.
Facilities:	[facility symbols] 
To Beach:	0.61 miles

CLEETHORPES – CLEETHORPES CENTRAL

Ginnies ★★★Guest Accommodation

27 Queen's Parade, Cleethorpes, Lincolnshire DN35 0DF

T:	+44 (0) 1472 694997
E:	enquiries@ginnies.co.uk
W:	ginnies.co.uk
Bedrooms:	7 • £36.00-£50.00 per double room per night, breakfast included
Open:	Seasonal opening – call for details
Description:	Homely and friendly, non-smoking guesthouse, close to seafront and amenities. Serves English, Continental and vegetarian specialist breakfasts.
Facilities:	
To Beach:	0.48 miles

CLEETHORPES – CLEETHORPES CENTRAL

Sherwood Guesthouse ♦♦♦Guest Accommodation

15 Kingsway, Cleethorpes, Lincolnshire, DN35 8QU

T:	+44 (0) 1472 692020
E:	sherwood.guesthouse@ntlworld.com
W:	sherwoodguesthouse.co.uk
Bedrooms:	6 • £50.00-£70.00 per double room per night, breakfast included • Debit/credit card accepted
Open:	Seasonal opening – call for details
Description:	Sherwood Guesthouse has en suite/standard rooms, most of which have superb views across the Humber estuary.
Facilities:	
To Beach:	0.34 miles

CLEETHORPES – CLEETHORPES CENTRAL

Thorpe Park Holiday Centre ★★★★Holiday Park

Thorpe Park Holiday Centre, Grimsby, DN36 0PW

T:	+44 (0) 1442 868325
E:	theresa.ludlow@bourne-leisure.co.uk
W:	british-holidays.co.uk
Pitches:	503 • £10.50-£30.50 per caravan per night • Debit/credit card accepted
Open:	Seasonal opening – call for details
Description:	Site 100 yards from the beach and two miles from Cleethorpes town centre. Lively family park with day- and night-time entertainment.
Facilities:	P
To Beach:	1.05 miles

CLEETHORPES – CLEETHORPES CENTRAL

Tudor Terrace Guesthouse ★★★★Guesthouse

11 Bradford Avenue, Cleethorpes, Lincolnshire DN35 0BB

T:	+44 (0) 1472 600800
E:	enquiries.tudorterrace@ntlworld.com
W:	tudorterrace.co.uk
Bedrooms:	1 • £58.00 per double room per night, breakfast included
Open:	Year round
Description:	Somewhere special – that's this black and white Victorian property. The rooms have en suite facilities, guest lounge, parking and private gardens.
Facilities:	
To Beach:	0.5 miles

SKEGNESS – TOWER ESPLANADE BEACH

Richmond Holiday Centre ★★★Holiday & Touring Park

Richmond Drive, Skegness, Lincolnshire, PE25 3TQ

T:	+44 (0) 1754 762097
E:	sales@richmondholidays.com
W:	richmondholidays.com
Pitches:	429 • £9.00-£16.00 per caravan per night • Debit/credit card; cheques/cash accepted
Open:	Seasonal opening – call for details
Description:	A level site, short walk from the town centre and beaches. Nightly entertainment during the peak weeks, leisure centre on site.
Facilities:	
To Beach:	0.91 miles

TRUSTHORPE – SUTTON ON SEA CENTRAL

Seacroft Holiday Estate ★★★Holiday & Touring Park

Sutton Road, Trusthorpe, Mablethorpe, Lincolnshire, LN12 2PN ROSE AWARD

T:	+44 (0) 1507 472421
E:	info@seacroftcaravanpark.co.uk
W:	seacroftcaravanpark.co.uk
Pitches:	51 • £11.00-£17.00 per caravan per night • Debit/credit card accepted
Open:	Seasonal opening – call for details
Description:	Situated directly on the coast between Mablethorpe and Sutton on Sea. An excellent caravan and chalet park with good facilities.
Facilities:	
To Beach:	0.92 miles

SOUTHPORT

Barford House Apartments ★★★/★Self Catering

32 Avondale Road, Merseyside, PR9 0ND

T: +44 (0) 1704 548119
E: barfordhs@aol.com
W: barfordhouse.co.uk

Units: 5 • £195.00-£795.00 per unit per week • Debit/credit card; cheques/cash accepted

Open: Year round except Christmas and New Year

Description: A fine, detached, Victorian house offering four spacious, self-contained, fully-equipped apartments with bath and shower, and two-, three- and four-bedroom houses.

Facilities: P

To Beach: 0.67 miles

SOUTHPORT

Beaucliffe Holiday Flats ★★★Self Catering

9 Leicester Street, Southport, PR9 0ER

T: +44 (0) 1704 537207
E: linda@beaucliffeholidayflats.co.uk
W: beaucliffeholidayflats.co.uk

Units: 2 • £240.00-£350.00 per unit per week • Cheques/cash accepted

Open: Seasonal opening – call for details

Description: Clean, friendly, self-catering holiday flats. Within five minutes' walk of Southport town centre. Just off the promenade.

Facilities: P TV

To Beach: 0.5 miles

EAST RUNTON – CROMER BEACH

Incleborough House Luxury B&B ★★★★★B&B

East Runton, Cromer, Norfolk, NR27 9PG

T: +44 (0) 1263 515939
E: enquiries@incleboroughhouse.co.uk
W: incleboroughhouse.co.uk

Bedrooms: 3 • £120.00-£150.00 per twin room per night, breakfast included • Debit/credit card accepted

Open: Year round

Description: Incleborough House is a stunning 17thC Norfolk country house, offering five star-luxury B&B all year round.

Facilities:

To Beach: 1.34 miles

NORFOLK

GREAT YARMOUTH – CENTRAL BEACH

Maluth Lodge ★★★★Guest Accommodation

40 North Denes Road, Great Yarmouth, Norfolk, NR30 4LU

T:	+44 (0) 1493 304652
E:	enquiries@maluthlodge.co.uk
W:	maluthlodge.co.uk
Bedrooms:	7 • £56.00-£80.00 per double room per night, breakfast included • Debit/credit card; cheques/cash accepted
Open:	Year round
Description:	Maluth Lodge is a premier, luxury guesthouse in the exclusive North Denes area, just a short walk to the beach, Venetian Waterways and boating lakes.
Facilities:	[illegible]
To Beach:	0.89 miles

SHERINGHAM

Viburnham House B&B ★★★★Guest Accommodation

Augusta Street, Sheringham, Norfolk, NR26 8LB SILVER AWARD

T:	+44 (0) 1263 822528
E:	viburnhamhouse@aol.com
W:	tiscover.co.uk/gb/guide/5gb,en/objectId,ACC15102gb/home.html
Bedrooms:	2 • £58.00 per twin room per night, room only
Open:	Year round
Description:	First class, en suite accommodation in a quiet, conservation area period house, close to beach, town centre and cliff walks.
Facilities:	[illegible]
To Beach:	0.18 miles

NORTHUMBERLAND

BAMBURGH

Burton Hall ♦♦♦♦Guest Accommodation

Bamburgh, Northumberland, NE69 7AR

T:	+44 (0) 1668 214213
E:	evehumphreys@aol.com
W:	burtonhall.co.uk
Bedrooms:	5 • £46.00-£80.00 per double room per night, breakfast included • Cheques/cash accepted
Open:	Seasonal opening – call for details
Description:	A spacious, elegant farmhouse offering friendly, homely accommodation in peaceful surroundings in the shadow of Bamburgh Castle.
Facilities:	[illegible]
To Beach:	1.41 miles

BAMBURGH

Castle View Bungalow

★★★★Self Catering

Booking: Springwood, South Lane, Seahouses, North Sunderland, NE68 7UL

T:	+44 (0) 1665 720320
E:	ian@slatehall.freeserve.co.uk
W:	slatehallridingcentre.com
Units:	1 • £245.00-£500.00 per unit per week • Debit/credit card; cheques/cash accepted
Open:	Year round
Description:	In the heart of Bamburgh with delightful views, overlooking fields to the front and Bamburgh Castle to the rear. Midweek and weekend breaks available during the winter months.
Facilities:	P
To Beach:	0.84 miles

BAMBURGH

Glenander B&B

★★★★B&B SILVER AWARD

27 Lucker Road, Bamburgh, Northumberland, NE69 7BS

T:	+44 (0) 1668 214336
E:	johntoland@tiscali.co.uk
W:	glenander.com
Bedrooms:	3 • £55.00-£100.00 per double room per night, breakfast included • Cheques/cash accepted
Open:	Seasonal opening – call for details
Description:	Glenander has three comfortable, double/twin rooms, which are available throughout the year. Amenities, hospitality trays, hairdryers and colour TV.
Facilities:	P TV
To Beach:	0.83 miles

BAMBURGH

Glororum Caravan Park

★★★Holiday, Touring & Camping Park

Glororum, Bamburgh, Northumberland, NE69 7AW

T:	+44 (0) 1668 214457
E:	info@glororum-caravanpark.co.uk
W:	glororum-caravanpark.co.uk
Pitches:	100 • £15.00-£17.00 per caravan per night • Debit/credit card accepted
Open:	Seasonal opening – call for details
Description:	Secluded and well-appointed farm site close to the coast and Bamburgh Castle. No caravans for hire.
Facilities:	P
To Beach:	1.77 miles

BAMBURGH

Point Cottages
★★★Self Catering

Booking: 30 The Oval, Benton, Newcastle upon Tyne, NE12 9PP

T:	+44 (0) 1912 662800
E:	info@bamburgh-cottages.co.uk
W:	bamburgh-cottages.co.uk
Units:	5 • £195.00-£485.00 per unit per week • Cheques/cash accepted
Open:	Year round
Description:	Cluster of cottages with sea views. Located next to golf course. Close to all amenities.
Facilities:	[illegible]
To Beach:	1.44 miles

BAMBURGH

Squirrel Cottage
★★★★B&B

1 Friars Court, Bamburgh, Northumberland, NE69 7AE

T:	+44 (0) 1668 214494
E:	theturnbulls2k@btinternet.com
W:	holidaynorthumbria.co.uk
Bedrooms:	3 • £60.00-£65.00 per double room per night, breakfast included • Cheques/cash accepted
Open:	Seasonal opening – call for details
Description:	Established, quality accommodation. All rooms with sea or castle view. A short stroll to either.
Facilities:	[illegible]
To Beach:	1.07 miles

BAMBURGH

Sunningdale Hotel
♦♦♦Guest Accommodation

21-23 Lucker Road, Bamburgh, Northumberland, NE69 7BS

T:	+44 (0) 1668 214334
E:	enquiries@sunningdale-hotel.com
W:	sunningdale-hotel.com
Bedrooms:	18 • £50.00-£90.00 per double room per night, breakfast included • Debit/credit card; cheques/cash accepted
Open:	Seasonal opening – call for details
Description:	A friendly, family-run hotel with all en suite bedrooms, plus a newly refurbished bar/lounge and restaurant specialising in delicious, home-made food.
Facilities:	[illegible]
To Beach:	0.83 miles

BAMBURGH

Victoria Hotel ★★Hotel

1 Front Street, Bamburgh, Northumberland, NE69 7BP

T:	+44 (0) 1668 214431
E:	enquiries@victoriahotel.net
W:	victoriahotel.net
Bedrooms:	29 • £94.00-£174.00 per double room per night, breakfast included • Debit/credit card; cheques/cash accepted
Open:	Seasonal opening – call for details
Description:	Stylish and welcoming hotel in romantic, coastal village setting. Award-winning brasserie. Comfortable, en suite bedrooms. Short breaks available.
Facilities:	[facility symbols]
To Beach:	0.83 miles

BEADNELL – BEADNELL BAY

Beach Court ♦♦♦♦♦Guest Accommodation

Harbour Road, Beadnell, NE67 5BJ SILVER AWARD

T:	+44 (0) 1665 720225
E:	info@beachcourt.com
W:	beachcourt.com
Bedrooms:	3 • £79.00 per double room per night, breakfast included • Debit/credit card; cheques/cash accepted
Open:	Year round except Christmas
Description:	Magnificent, beach-side home offering an atmosphere of timeless tranquillity. Secure courtyard parking. Non-smokers only. Winner: Pride of Northumbria. Featured in *Sunday Times'* Top 20 British Seaside Hotels.
Facilities:	[facility symbols]
To Beach:	0.49 miles

BEADNELL – BEADNELL BAY

Beadnell House ★★★★Guest Accommodation

Beadnell, Chathill, NE67 5AT

T:	+44 (0) 1665 721380
E:	info@beadnellhouse.com
W:	beadnellhouse.com
Bedrooms:	11 • £70.00-£110.00 per double room per night, breakfast included • Debit/credit card accepted
Open:	Seasonal opening – call for details
Description:	Grand country house minutes from beach. Ideal tourist and sporting base. Lounge, bar and hearty breakfasts. Evening meals, Friday-Tuesday from £17.
Facilities:	[facility symbols]
To Beach:	0.61 miles

BEADNELL – BEADNELL BAY

Low Dover Beadnell Bay ♦♦♦♦Guest Accommodation

Harbour Road, Beadnell, Chathill, NE67 5BJ
GOLD AWARD

T:	+44 (0) 1665 720291
E:	enquiries@lowdover.co.uk
W:	lowdover.co.uk
Bedrooms:	3 • £60.00-£98.00 per double room per night, breakfast included • Debit/credit card; cheques/cash accepted
Open:	Year round
Description:	Virtually encompassed by the sea, restful seashore accommodation with ground floor suites. Enjoy breakfast with sea views. Beautiful garden. Recommended by *Which? Good B&B Guide*.
Facilities:	
To Beach:	0.49 miles

EMBLETON – LOW NEWTON BEACH

Dunstanburgh Castle Hotel ★★Hotel

Embleton, Alnwick, NE66 3UN

T:	+44 (0) 1665 576111
E:	stay@dunstanburghcastlehotel.co.uk
W:	dunstanburghcastlehotel.co.uk
Bedrooms:	20 • £59.00-£97.00 per double room per night, breakfast included • Debit/credit card; cheques/cash accepted
Open:	Seasonal opening – call for details
Description:	High standards and excellent facilities with the added warmth of a family-run hotel. Two fine restaurants. Close to beach.
Facilities:	
To Beach:	1.31 miles

EMBLETON – LOW NEWTON BEACH

Rose Cottages ★★★★Self Catering

Embleton, Alnwick, NE66 3UN

T:	+44 (0) 1665 576111
E:	stay@dunstanburghcastlehotel.co.uk
W:	dunstanburghcastlehotel.co.uk
Units:	3 • £200.00-£400.00 per unit per week • Debit/credit card; cheques/cash accepted
Open:	Seasonal opening – call for details
Description:	Luxurious barn conversions in picturesque, desirable village. Character features, open fires, modern bathroom and kitchens. Minutes from magnificent beach.
Facilities:	
To Beach:	1.33 miles

NEWTON-BY-THE-SEA – LOW NEWTON

Newton Hall Caravan Park ★★★Holiday & Touring Park

Newton-by-the-Sea, Alnwick, NE66 3DZ

T:	+44 (0) 1665 576239
E:	patterson@newtonholidays.co.uk
W:	newtonholidays.co.uk
Pitches:	33 • £13.00-£18.00 per caravan per night • Debit/credit card; cheques/cash accepted
Open:	Seasonal opening – call for details
Description:	Small, coastal park close to beaches and golf course. Set in the grounds of the 18thC Newton Hall. Only nine miles from the famous Alnwick Castle Gardens.
Facilities:	
To Beach:	0.63 miles

NEWTON-BY-THE-SEA – LOW NEWTON

Newton Hall Cottages ★★★/★Self Catering

Newton-by-the-Sea, Alnwick, NE66 3DZ

T:	+44 (0) 1665 576239
E:	patterson@newtonholidays.co.uk
W:	newtonholidays.co.uk
Units:	3 • £285.00-£535.00 per unit per week • Debit/credit card; cheques/cash accepted
Open:	Year round
Description:	Spacious Georgian accommodation with two acres of gardens. Ideal base to enjoy magnificent coastline, Alnwick Castle and Gardens and panoramic countryside.
Facilities:	
To Beach:	0.63 miles

NORTH SUNDERLAND – ST AIDANS BEACH

Longstone House Hotel ★★Hotel

182 Main Street, North Sunderland, Seahouses, NE68 7UA

T:	+44 (0) 1665 720212
E:	info@longstonehousehotel.co.uk
W:	longstonehousehotel.co.uk
Bedrooms:	17 • £52.00-£80.00 per double room per night, breakfast included • Debit/credit card; cheques/cash accepted
Open:	Seasonal opening – call for details
Description:	Set in the heart of the Old Village, close to beaches and the fishing harbour and within view of Bamburgh Castle and the sea. Renowned for good food and friendly service.
Facilities:	
To Beach:	0.79 miles

NORTH SUNDERLAND – ST AIDANS BEACH

Railston House ★★★★Guest Accommodation

133 Main Street, North Sunderland, Seahouses, NE68 7TS SILVER AWARD

T:	+44 (0) 1665 720912
E:	twgrundy@btinternet.com
W:	railstonhouse.com
Bedrooms:	3 • £58.00-£70.00 per double room per night, breakfast included
Open:	Seasonal opening – call for details
Description:	A late Georgian house, maintained and furnished to a high standard offering peace and tranquillity to guests.
Facilities:	[illegible]
To Beach:	0.79 miles

NORTH SUNDERLAND – ST AIDANS BEACH

Springwood ★★★★B&B

South Lane, North Sunderland, Seahouses, NE68 7UL

T:	+44 (0) 1665 720320
E:	marian@slatehall.freeserve.co.uk
W:	slatehallridingcentre.com
Bedrooms:	3 • £60.00-£70.00 per double room per night, breakfast included • Cheques/cash accepted
Open:	Seasonal opening – call for details
Description:	Springwood is situated in 68 acres on perimeter of Seahouses, panoramic views, delicious breakfasts. Bamburgh Castle, Farne Islands, Lindisfarne, Cheviot Hills all nearby.
Facilities:	[illegible]
To Beach:	0.82 miles

NORTH SUNDERLAND – ST AIDANS

The Old Manse ★★★★B&B

9 North Lane, North Sunderland, Seahouses, NE68 7UQ

T:	+44 (0) 1665 720521
E:	info@theoldemanse.com
W:	theoldemanse.com
Bedrooms:	3 • £56.00-£60.00 per double room per night, breakfast included • Debit/credit card accepted
Open:	Seasonal opening – call for details
Description:	A character, period guesthouse, quietly tucked away in a historic part of Seahouses – easy walking distance of village, harbour and beach. Comfortable, en suite guest rooms offering a high standard of accommodation. Off-road parking.
Facilities:	[illegible]
To Beach:	0.72 miles

SEAHOUSES – ST AIDANS BEACH

Bamburgh Castle Hotel

★★★Hotel

Seahouses, Northumberland, NE68 7SQ

T:	+44 (0) 1665 720283
E:	bamburghcastlehotel@btinternet.com
W:	bamburghcastlehotel.co.uk
Bedrooms:	20 • £83.90-£104.00 per double room per night, breakfast included • Debit/credit card; cheques/cash accepted
Open:	Year round except Christmas
Description:	Overlooking the harbour with magnificent views of the Farne Islands, Bamburgh Castle and Holy Island. Log fire in lounges, private garden and secure car parking.
Facilities:	
To Beach:	0.77 miles

SEAHOUSES – ST AIDANS BEACH

Beach House Hotel

★★Hotel

Seafront, 12a St Aidans, Seahouses, NE68 7SR

T:	+44 (0) 1665 720337
E:	enq@beachhousehotel.co.uk
W:	beachhousehotel.co.uk
Bedrooms:	14 • £74.00-£108.00 per double room per night, breakfast included • Debit/credit card; cheques/cash accepted
Open:	Seasonal opening – call for details
Description:	Quiet, comfortable and friendly, family-run hotel overlooking the Farne Islands, specialising in imaginative home cooking and baking. Especially suited to those seeking a peaceful holiday. The property is a non-smoking establishment.
Facilities:	
To Beach:	0.5 miles

SEAHOUSES – ST AIDANS BEACH

Olde Ship Hotel

★★Hotel
SILVER AWARD

Main Street, Seahouses, Northumberland, NE68 7RD

T:	+44 (0) 1665 720200
E:	theoldeship@seahouses.co.uk
W:	seahouses.co.uk
Bedrooms:	18 • £96.00-£110.00 per double room per night, breakfast included • Debit/credit card accepted
Open:	Seasonal opening – call for details
Description:	Hotel with a long-established reputation for good food and drink in comfortably relaxing, old-fashioned surroundings.
Facilities:	
To Beach:	0.82 miles

SEAHOUSES – ST AIDANS BEACH

Sharrow

♦♦♦♦Guest Accommodation
SILVER AWARD

98 Main Street, Seahouses, Northumberland, NE68 7TP

T:	+44 (0) 1665 721794
E:	enquiry@sharrow-seahouses.co.uk
W:	sharrow-seahouses.co.uk
Bedrooms:	2 • £55.00-£70.00 per double room per night, breakfast included • Debit/credit card accepted
Open:	Seasonal opening – call for details
Description:	Furnished to a high standard. Ideally situated for exploring coast, borders, Alnwick Garden and Farne Islands. Great local food.
Facilities:	
To Beach:	0.79 miles

SEAHOUSES – ST AIDANS BEACH

Springhill Farm

★★★★/★Self Catering

Seahouses, Northumberland, NE68 7UR

T:	+44 (0) 1665 721820
E:	enquiries@springhill-farm.co.uk
W:	springhill-farm.co.uk
Units:	6 • £195.00-£1,600.00 per unit per week • Debit/credit card; cheques/cash accepted
Open:	Seasonal opening – call for details
Description:	Peacefully situated property, close to the beautiful coast of Northumberland. With panoramic views of the Farne Islands, Bamburgh Castle and Cheviot Hills.
Facilities:	P
To Beach:	0.67 miles

WARKWORTH

The Old Manse

♦♦♦♦Guest Accommodation

20 The Butts, Warkworth, Morpeth NE65 0SS

T:	+44 (0) 1665 710850
E:	a.coulter1@btinternet.com
W:	oldmanse.info
Bedrooms:	2 • £54.00-£60.00 per double room per night, breakfast included
Open:	Year round except Christmas and New Year
Description:	The Old Manse is a Grade II Listed building built in 1845. Accommodation is spacious, private, quiet, convenient and interesting.
Facilities:	
To Beach:	1.17 miles

BREAN

Diamond Farm ★★★Camping & Touring Park

Weston Road, Brean, Nr Burnham-on-Sea, Somerset, TA8 2RL

T: +44 (0) 1278 751263
E: trevor@diamondfarm42.freeserve.co.uk
W: diamondfarm.co.uk

Pitches: 151 • £3.50-£10.00 per caravan per night

Open: Seasonal opening – call for details

Description: Quiet, family site alongside River Axe and five minutes from beach. Fishing on site. Close to main coast road and beach.

Facilities:

To Beach: 0.5 miles

BREAN

Northam Farm Touring Park ★★★★Holiday, Touring & Camping Park

South Road, Brean, Burnham-on-Sea, Somerset, TA8 2SE

T: +44 (0) 1278 751244
E: enquiries@northamfarm.co.uk
W: northamfarm.co.uk

Pitches: 950 • £5.50-£17.50 per caravan per night • Debit/credit card; cheques/cash accepted

Open: Seasonal opening – call for details

Description: Spacious surrounds and lovely views of the Mendips, two minutes' walk from five miles of sandy beach. Choice of grass or hardstanding pitches.

Facilities:

To Beach: 0.1 miles

BREAN

The Old Rectory Motel ♦♦♦♦Guest Accommodation

Church Road, Brean, Burnham-on-Sea, Somerset, TA8 2SF

T: +44 (0) 1278 751447
E: helen@old-rectory.fsbusiness.co.uk
W: old-rectory.fsbusiness.co.uk

Bedrooms: 10 • £45.00-£50.00 per double room per night, breakfast included • Debit/credit card accepted

Open: Year round

Description: Ground floor, en suite accommodation suitable for all – converted from old carriage house and school room.

Facilities:

To Beach: 0.28 miles

SOMERSET

BREAN

Warren Farm Holiday Centre

★★★★Holiday, Touring & Camping Park

Warren Road, Brean Sands, Burnham-on-Sea, Somerset, TA8 2RP

T:	+44 (0) 1278 751227
E:	enquiries@warren-farm.co.uk
W:	warren-farm.co.uk
Pitches:	574 • £6.00-£13.00 per caravan per night • Debit/credit card accepted
Open:	Seasonal opening – call for details
Description:	Large, family site near sandy beaches. Indoor and outdoor play equipment and fishing facilities feature strongly. Also near is the Beachcomber Inn.
Facilities:	
To Beach:	0.73 miles

BURNHAM-ON-SEA

Knights Rest

♦♦♦Guest Accommodation

9 Dunstan Road, Burnham-on-Sea, Somerset, TA8 1ER

T:	+44 (0) 1278 782318
E:	enquiries@knightsrest.net
W:	knightsrest.net/
Bedrooms:	5 • £40.00-£50.00 per double room per night, breakfast included
Open:	Year round
Description:	A quiet, family-run home in an Edwardian townhouse. Four minutes from the beach and shops, an easy walk.
Facilities:	
To Beach:	0.36 miles

BURNHAM-ON-SEA

St Aubyns Guesthouse

★★★★Guesthouse

11 Berrow Road, Burnham-on-Sea, Somerset, TA8 2ET

T:	+44 (0) 1278 773769
E:	markhowes@stevejefferies.fsnet.co.uk
W:	staubyns-guesthouse.co.uk
Bedrooms:	6 • £45.00-£50.00 per double room per night, breakfast included
Open:	Year round except Christmas and New Year
Description:	A privately-owned guesthouse with a reputation for a friendly atmosphere. An ideal place to relax and unwind.
Facilities:	
To Beach:	0.12 miles

BURNHAM-ON-SEA

The Warren Guesthouse
★★★★Guesthouse

29 Berrow Road, Burnham-on-Sea, Somerset, TA8 2EZ

T:	+44 (0) 1278 786726
E:	info@thewarrenguesthouse.co.uk
W:	Thewarrenguesthouse.co.uk
Bedrooms:	6 • £42.00-£45.00 per double room per night, breakfast included • Debit/credit card; cheques/cash accepted
Open:	Year round except Christmas and New Year
Description:	A spacious, attractive, licensed Victorian building with large gardens within easy reach of town centre, golf course and beach.
Facilities:	
To Beach:	0.26 miles

HIGHBRIDGE – BURNHAM-ON-SEA BEACH

Greenacre Place Touring Caravan Park and Holiday Cottage
★★★★Touring Park

Bristol Road, Edithmead, Highbridge, Somerset, TA9 4HA

T:	+44 (0) 1278 785227
E:	sm.alderton@btopenworld.com
W:	greenacreplace.com
Pitches:	21 • £8.50-£11.00 per caravan per night
Open:	Year round except Christmas and New Year
Description:	Small, level caravan park with easy access, ideally placed for touring Somerset. Holiday cottages also on site.
Facilities:	P
To Beach:	1.84 miles

HIGHBRIDGE – BURNHAM-ON-SEA BEACH

Home Farm Holiday Park
★★★★★Holiday & Touring Park

Edithmead, Highbridge, Somerset, TA9 4HD

T:	+44 (0) 1278 788888
E:	office@homefarmholidaypark.co.uk
W:	homefarmholidaypark.co.uk
Pitches:	1202 • £7.00-£18.50 per caravan per night • Debit/credit card accepted
Open:	Year round except Christmas
Description:	Five-star touring site, close to motorway with excellent holiday homes available to purchase. Open 11 months of the year.
Facilities:	P
To Beach:	1.52 miles

UPHILL – BREAN COVE

The Old Hall
★★★Guesthouse

88 Uphill Way, Uphill, Weston-Super-Mare, BS23 4X

T:	+44 (0) 1934 629970
E:	oldhallmail@yahoo.co.uk
W:	theoldhalluphill.co.uk
Bedrooms:	5 • £55.00 per double room per night, breakfast included • Debit/credit card accepted
Open:	Year round except Christmas and New Year
Description:	Warm and friendly, family-run guesthouse in the charming village of Uphill. En suite bedrooms furnished and maintained to a high standard.
Facilities:	
To Beach:	1.16 miles

WESTON-SUPER-MARE

Cornerways
♦♦♦Guest Accommodation

14 Whitecross Road, Weston-super-Mare, Somerset, BS23 1EW

T:	+44 (0) 1934 623708
E:	cornerwaysgh@aol.com
W:	cornerwaysweston.com
Bedrooms:	4 • £44.00-£54.00 per double room per night, breakfast included • Cheques/cash accepted
Open:	Year round except Christmas and New Year
Description:	Two-storey, stone-built guesthouse, in corner site with car park and well-kept gardens, close to shops and a few minutes from railway station.
Facilities:	
To Beach:	0.25 miles

WESTON-SUPER-MARE

Saxonia Guesthouse
★★★Guesthouse

95 Locking Road, Weston-super-Mare, Somerset, BS23 3EW

T:	+44 (0) 1934 424850
E:	saxoniahotel@btinternet.com
W:	saxoniaguesthouse.co.uk
Bedrooms:	9 • £50.00-£70.00 per double room per night, room only • Debit/credit card; cheques/cash accepted
Open:	Seasonal opening – call for details
Description:	Friendly, family-run guesthouse near beach, 15 minutes from seafront and Sealife Centre. All rooms en suite (one on ground floor). Shower, hairdryer and colour TV in all rooms.
Facilities:	P
To Beach:	0.79 miles

WESTON-SUPER-MARE

Spreyton Guesthouse ★★★Guesthouse

72 Locking Road, Weston-super-Mare, Somerset, BS23 3EN

T: +44 (0) 1934 416887
E: Info@spreytonguesthouse.fsnet.co.uk
W: spreytonguesthouse.com

Bedrooms: 6 • £38.00-£48.00 per double room per night, breakfast included • Debit/credit card accepted

Open: Year round except Christmas and New Year

Description: Pleasant, friendly, family guesthouse with own car park. Easy, level walk to seafront and amenities. Reasonable rates. Family rooms available.

Facilities: P

To Beach: 0.78 miles

WESTON-SUPER-MARE

The Grand Atlantic ♦♦♦♦Guest Accommodation

Beach Road, Weston-super-Mare, Somerset, BS23 1BA

T: +44 (0) 1942 824824
E: reservations@washearings.com
W: washearings.com

Bedrooms: 70 • £27.00-£48.00 per double room per night, room only • Debit/credit card; cheques/cash accepted

Open: Year round

Description: A traditional Victorian seaside hotel built on Weston's famous promenade. Weston's huge sandy beach and grand pier make it a popular destination. Entertainment with a host every night.

Facilities: P

To Beach: 0.2 miles

SOUTHWOLD – SOUTHWOLD PIER BEACH

The Swan Hotel ★★★Hotel

Market Place, Southwold, IP18 6EG — SILVER AWARD

T: +44 (0) 1502 722186
E: swan.reception@adnams.co.uk
W: tiscover.co.uk/gb/guide/5gb,en/objectId,ACC14669gb/home.html

Bedrooms: 1 • £150.00 per double room per night, breakfast included • Debit/credit card accepted

Open: Year round

Description: A classic, seaside hotel situated on the Suffolk heritage coast. A delightful location, relaxing ambiance, delicious food and serious wine list.

Facilities:

To Beach: 0.41 miles

BEXHILL-ON-SEA

Buenos Aires Guesthouse

♦♦♦♦Guest Accommodation

24 Albany Road, Bexhill-on-Sea, East Sussex, TN40 1BZ

T:	+44 (0) 1424 212269
E:	buenosairesguest@hotmail.com
W:	buenosairesguesthouse.com
Bedrooms:	7 • £45.00-£55.00 per double room per night, breakfast included
Open:	Year round except Christmas and New Year
Description:	Well established guesthouse. Family-run, centrally situated and adjacent to the seafront, De La Warr Pavilion and the Town Centre. High standards in a warm, friendly atmosphere.
Facilities:	[facility symbols]
To Beach:	0.25 miles

BEXHILL-ON-SEA

Hotel Dunselma

♦♦♦♦Guest Accommodation

Bexhill-on-Sea, East Sussex, TN40 1BP

T:	+44 (0) 1424 734144
E:	stay@dunselma.co.uk
W:	dunselma.co.uk
Bedrooms:	8 • £60.00-£65.00 per double room per night, breakfast included • Debit/credit card accepted
Open:	Seasonal opening – call for details
Description:	Hotel Dunselma is opposite the De La Warr Pavilion. Once a fashionable seafront Edwardian townhouse, it is now run as a guesthouse.
Facilities:	[facility symbols]
To Beach:	0.17 miles

BEXHILL-ON-SEA

Park Lodge

★★★★Guest Accommodation

16 Egerton Road, Bexhill-on-Sea, East Sussex, TN39 3HH

T:	+44 (0) 1424 216547
E:	info@parklodgehotel.co.uk
W:	parklodgehotel.co.uk
Bedrooms:	10 • £54.00 per double room per night, breakfast included • Debit/credit card accepted
Open:	Seasonal opening – call for details
Description:	Park Lodge is an informal, family-run hotel close to the promenade and sea, and situated centrally for restaurants, shops and the De La Warr Pavilion.
Facilities:	[facility symbols]
To Beach:	0.32 miles

BEXHILL-ON-SEA

The Northern Hotel

★★Hotel

74-78 Sea Road, Bexhill-on-Sea, East Sussex, TN40 1JN

T: +44 (0) 1424 212836
E: reception@northernhotel.co.uk
W: northernhotel.co.uk

Bedrooms: 8 • £69.00 per double room per night, breakfast included • Debit/credit card accepted

Open: Year round except Christmas and New Year

Description: The Northern Hotel has been developed and improved by the Sims family for 48 years. All rooms are delightfully furnished and have en suite facilities, central heating, remote control colour TV, direct-dial telephone and beverage tray.

Facilities:

To Beach: 0.05 miles

CAMBER – CAMBER SANDS

Camber Sands Holiday Park

★★★★Holiday Park
ROSE AWARD

New Lydd Road, Camber, Rye, TN31 7RT

T: +44 (0) 871 664 9718
E: holidaysales.cambersands@park-resorts.com
W: park-resorts.com

Pitches: 225 • £20.00-£25.00 per caravan per night • Debit/credit card accepted

Open: Seasonal opening – call for details

Description: Camber Sands is a winning holiday park for all the family. Adjacent to seven miles of award-winning Blue Flag beach you can explore the scenic Sussex countryside, 1066 country and historic towns such as Rye and Winchelsea.

Facilities: P

To Beach: 0.64 miles

CAMBER – CAMBER SANDS

The Place Camber Sands

♦♦♦♦Guest Accommodation

The Place Camber Sands, Camber, East Sussex, TN31 7RB

T: +44 (0) 1797 225057
E: enquiries@theplacecambersands.co.uk
W: theplacecambersands.co.uk

Bedrooms: 18 • £75.00-£100.00 per double room per night, breakfast included • Debit/credit card accepted

Open: Seasonal opening – call for details

Description: A stylish hotel, brasserie and conference facility. The bedrooms are all en suite with TV/DVD combination units, digital radios, hairdryers and tea-/coffee-making facilities.

Facilities: P

To Beach: 0.26 miles

EASTBOURNE – PIER TO WISH TOWER

Best Western Lansdowne Hotel ★★★Hotel

Lansdowne Terrace, King Edwards Parade, Eastbourne, BN21 4EE SILVER AWARD

T: +44 (0) 1323 725174
E: reception@lansdowne-hotel.co.uk
W: bw-lansdownehotel.co.uk

Bedrooms: 101 • £92.00-£141.00 per double room per night, breakfast included • Debit/credit card accepted

Open: Seasonal opening – call for details

Description: Traditional, seafront hotel overlooking the Western Lawns and the Wish Tower. Theatres and shops three-four minutes' walk away. A total of 25 non-smoking rooms. Daily changing menus together with a choice of a la carte dishes.

Facilities:

To Beach: 0.31 miles

EASTBOURNE – PIER TO WISH TOWER

Burlington Hotel ♦♦♦♦Guest Accommodation

Grand Parade, Eastbourne, BN21 3YN

T: +44 (0) 1323 722724
E: gm.bur@shearingsholidays.co.uk
W: shearingsholidays.com

Bedrooms: 163 • £60.00-£96.00 per double room per night, breakfast included • Debit/credit card; cheques/cash accepted

Open: Year round

Description: Burlington Hotel's Grade II Listed building facade and elegant interior enjoys a popular location overlooking the famous carpet gardens and pier.

Facilities:

To Beach: 0.13 miles

EASTBOURNE – PIER TO WISH TOWER

Carlton Court Hotel ★★Hotel

10 Wilmington Square, Eastbourne, BN21 4EA

T: +44 (0) 1323 430668
E: carlton@carltoncourthotel.co.uk
W: carltoncourthotel.co.uk

Bedrooms: 27 • £54.00-£90.00 per double room per night, breakfast included • Debit/credit card accepted

Open: Year round

Description: In one of the finest positions overlooking the gardens in Wilmington Square, within yards of the sea and close to the Winter Gardens, Congress and Devonshire Park Theatres.

Facilities:

To Beach: 0.28 miles

EASTBOURNE – PIER TO WISH TOWER

Congress Hotel ★★Hotel

31-41 Carlisle Road, Eastbourne, BN21 4JS

T: +44 (0) 1323 732118
E: reservations@congresshotel.co.uk
W: congresshotel.co.uk

Bedrooms: 61 • £64.00-£160.00 per double room per night, breakfast included • Debit/credit card accepted

Open: Year round

Description: Family-run hotel ideally situated close to seafront, theatres and town centre. We have our own car park and unrestricted street parking. All rooms are en suite.

Facilities: ◐P

To Beach: 0.34 miles

EASTBOURNE – PIER TO WISH TOWER

Cromwell Private Hotel ★★★★Guest Accommodation

23 Cavendish Place, Eastbourne, BN21 3EJ

T: +44 (0) 1323 725288
E: info@cromwellhotel.co.uk
W: cromwellhotel.co.uk

Bedrooms: 8 • £52.00-£60.00 per double room per night, breakfast included • Debit/credit card accepted

Open: Year round

Description: Built in 1851 as an elegant townhouse for middle class Victorians. It has been taking paying guests for more than 90 years. The lounge has its original marble fire surround.

Facilities: P

To Beach: 0.29 miles

EASTBOURNE – PIER TO WISH TOWER

Cumberland Hotel ★★★Hotel

34-36 Grand Parade, Eastbourne, East Sussex, BN21 3YT

T: +44 (0) 1323 730342
E: reservations@hotelcumberland.co.uk
W: hotelcumberland.co.uk

Bedrooms: 9 • £80.00-£100.00 per double room per night, breakfast included • Debit/credit card accepted

Open: Year round

Description: Wonderful seafront position opposite the bandstand. Elegant foyer and lounges. Breathtaking seaview restaurant. Sprung dance floor ballroom. Close to town centre and all theatres. Lift to all floors. Perfect for all functions.

Facilities: ◐P

To Beach: 0 miles

EASTBOURNE – PIER TO WISH TOWER

Grand Hotel ★★★★★Hotel

King Edwards Parade, Eastbourne, BN21 4EQ GOLD AWARD

T: +44 (0) 1323 412345
E: reservations@grandeastbourne.com
W: grandeastbourne.com

Bedrooms: 152 • £130.00-£197.00 per double room per night, breakfast included • Debit/credit card accepted

Open: Year round

Description: England's finest resort hotel – as described by the RAC. 152 bedrooms and suites, dramatic public areas including two restaurants and luxurious lounges. Facilities include a comprehensive health club with hair and beauty salon.

Facilities:

To Beach: 0.44 miles

EASTBOURNE – PIER TO WISH TOWER

Little Foxes B&B ♦♦♦♦Guest Accommodation

24 Wannock Road, Eastbourne, BN22 7JU

T: +44 (0) 1323 640670
E: GunnerSmith2001@yahoo.co.uk
W: thelittlefoxes.com

Bedrooms: 2 • £46.00-£54.00 per twin room per night, breakfast included

Open: Year round

Description: Near Princes Park and seafront. Quiet road, parking. Hairdryer, ironing board and iron available, flexible breakfast times (7.00-9.30am). Packed lunches available.

Facilities: P

To Beach: 1.22 miles

EASTBOURNE – PIER TO WISH TOWER

Oban Hotel ★★Hotel

King Edwards Parade, Eastbourne, BN21 4DS

T: +44 (0) 1323 731581
E: info@oban-hotel.co.uk
W: oban-hotel.co.uk

Bedrooms: 31 • £68.00-£80.00 per double room per night, breakfast included • Debit/credit card accepted

Open: Year round

Description: The Oban is on Eastbourne's elegant seafront, within easy walking distance to the main theatres and other attractions.

Facilities: P

To Beach: 0.2 miles

EASTBOURNE – PIER TO WISH TOWER

St Omer Hotel
★★★★Guesthouse

13 Royal Parade, Eastbourne, BN22 7AR

T: +44 (0) 1323 722152
E: stomerhotel@hotmail.com
W: st-omer.co.uk

Bedrooms: 7 • £50.00-£60.00 per double room per night, breakfast included • Debit/credit card accepted

Open: Year round

Description: The proprietors welcome you to the St Omer which is located on the seafront and has panoramic views of the sea, beach and promenade from the sun-lounge and front bedrooms.

Facilities:

To Beach: 0.5 miles

EASTBOURNE – HOLYWELL BEACH

Hydro Hotel
★★★Hotel
SILVER AWARD

Mount Road, Eastbourne, BN20 7HZ

T: +44 (0) 1323 720643
E: sales@hydrohotel.com
W: hydrohotel.com

Bedrooms: 32 • £90.00-£130.00 per double room per night, breakfast included • Debit/credit card accepted

Open: Year round

Description: Situated on the South Cliff, the hotel enjoys spectacular sea views from a unique garden setting. The outdoor pool, putting and croquet are always popular in the summer.

Facilities: P

To Beach: 0.68 miles

HASTINGS – NORMANS BAY BEACH

Lansdowne Hotel
★★Hotel

1 & 2 Robertson Terrace, Hastings, TN34 1JE

T: +44 (0) 800 7318 79501424429605
E: info@lansdowne-hotel.com
W: lansdowne-hotel.com

Bedrooms: 31 • £70.00-£89.00 per double room per night, breakfast included • Debit/credit card accepted

Open: Year round

Description: Ideally situated in a central position on the seafront, with the pier and a long promenade to the right; to the left is the historic Old Town with its fishing quarter and unique net huts, plus winding streets full of unusual twists and turns.

Facilities:

To Beach: 0.5 miles

PEVENSEY BAY

Bay View Park ★★★Holiday, Touring & Camping Park

Old Martello Road, Pevensey Bay, Pevensey, BN24 6DX

T:	+44 (0) 1323 768688
E:	holidays@bay-view.co.uk
W:	bay-view.co.uk
Pitches:	84 • £12.00-£15.00 per caravan per night • Cheques/cash accepted
Open:	Seasonal opening – call for details
Description:	Family site on a private road next to the beach. Play area. Showers and laundry. Small, well-stocked shop. Ideal touring base.
Facilities:	
To Beach:	0.85 miles

SEAFORD

Tudor Manor Hotel ♦♦♦♦Guest Accommodation

Eastbourne Road, Seaford, BN25 4DB SILVER AWARD

T:	+44 (0) 1323 896006
E:	tudormanorhl@aol.com
W:	tudormanor.co.uk
Bedrooms:	5 • £70.00-£120.00 per double room per night, breakfast included • Debit/credit card; cheques/cash accepted
Open:	Year round
Description:	Beautiful manor-house set in landscaped gardens, luxurious accommodation. A four-poster suite available with private bathroom. Bar.
Facilities:	
To Beach:	1.14 miles

ST LEONARDS-ON-SEA – NORMANS BAY

Grand Hotel ♦♦♦Guest Accommodation

Grand Parade, St Leonards-on-Sea, TN38 0DD

T:	+44 (0) 1401 4244 28510
E:	petermann@grandhotelhastings.co.uk
W:	grandhotelhastings.co.uk
Bedrooms:	20 • £40.00-£70.00 per double room per night, breakfast included
Open:	Year round except Christmas and New Year
Description:	This well-established, prime, seafront hotel, just half a mile from Hastings Pier and only 10 minutes' walk from Warrior Square station, welcomes everyone, including children. Unrestricted and disabled parking in front of the hotel.
Facilities:	
To Beach:	0.31 miles

ST LEONARDS-ON-SEA – NORMANS BAY

Marina Lodge ♦♦♦Guest Accommodation

123 Marina, St Leonards-on-Sea, TN38 0BN

T:	+44 (0) 1424 715067
E:	marinalodgeguesthse@tiscali.co.uk
W:	marinalodge.co.uk
Bedrooms:	7 • £36.00-£60.00 per double room per night, breakfast included • Debit/credit card accepted
Open:	Year round
Description:	A well-established guesthouse on the seafront. En suite rooms have sea view. All have colour TV, tea-/ coffee-making facilities, hot/cold water and central heating. Lounge for guests' use. Special diets catered for.
Facilities:	
To Beach:	0.93 miles

ST LEONARDS-ON-SEA – NORMANS BAY

Seaspray Guesthouse ★★★★Guest Accommodation

54 Eversfield Place, St Leonards-on-Sea, TN37 6DB

T:	+44 (0) 1424 436583
E:	jo@seaspraybb.co.uk
W:	seaspraybb.co.uk
Bedrooms:	10 • £50.00 per double room per night, breakfast included
Open:	Year round
Description:	Seaspray is a spacious, Victorian, family-run B&B recently refurbished to a very high standard. Situated on the promenade 100 metres west of pier. Front of the house has panoramic views of the seafront and the English Channel.
Facilities:	
To Beach:	0.1 miles

ST LEONARDS-ON-SEA – NORMANS BAY

Sherwood Guesthouse ★★★★Guesthouse

15 Grosvenor Crescent, St Leonards-on-Sea, TN38 0AA

T:	+44 (0) 1424 433331
E:	wendy@sherwoodhastings.co.uk
W:	sherwoodhastings.co.uk
Bedrooms:	9 • £50.00-£60.00 per double room per night, breakfast included • Debit/credit card accepted
Open:	Seasonal opening – call for details
Description:	A warm welcome awaits you at this Victorian, non-smoking guesthouse which offers high standards of comfort and cleanliness. All rooms are newly decorated with lots of personal touches. There is free, off-road parking. Enjoy a full or vegetarian breakfast.
Facilities:	
To Beach:	1.18 miles

WINCHELSEA

Winchelsea Lodge Motel ♦♦♦♦Guest Accommodation

Winchelsea Lodge Motel, Hastings Road, Winchelsea, TN36 4AD

T:	+44 (0) 1797 226211
E:	rooms@1066motels.co.uk
W:	1066motels.co.uk
Bedrooms:	24 • £45.00 per double room per night, room only • Debit/ credit card accepted
Open:	Year round
Description:	The Lodge is nestled unobtrusively alongside the main A259 Hastings to Rye road, blending into the beautiful rural countryside of one of the cinque ports towns – Winchelsea.
Facilities:	[illegible]
To Beach:	1.23 miles

BOGNOR REGIS – EAST OF THE PIER

Beachcroft Hotel Spa & Restaurant ★★Hotel

Clyde Road, Felpham, Bognor Regis, West Sussex, PO22 7AH

T:	+44 (0) 1243 827142
E:	reservations@beachcroft-hotel.co.uk
W:	beachcroft-hotel.co.uk
Bedrooms:	34 • £58.00-£65.00 per double room per night, breakfast included • Debit/credit card accepted
Open:	Seasonal opening – call for details
Description:	The Beachcroft enjoys an excellent reputation for quality accommodation, fine cuisine and personal hospitality.
Facilities:	[illegible]
To Beach:	0.75 miles

BOGNOR REGIS – EAST OF THE PIER

Regis Lodge ♦♦♦Guest Accommodation

3 Gloucester Road, Bognor Regis, West Sussex, PO21 1NU

T:	+44 (0) 1243 827110
E:	frank@regislodge.co.uk
W:	regislodge.co.uk
Bedrooms:	8 • £50.00-£70.00 per double room per night, breakfast included
Open:	Year round except Christmas and New Year
Description:	A warm welcome awaits you at this friendly guesthouse in sunny Bognor Regis. Our beds are comfortable and our breakfasts are great!
Facilities:	[illegible]
To Beach:	0.25 miles

BOGNOR REGIS – EAST OF THE PIER

Swan Guesthouse ♦♦♦♦Guest Accommodation

17 Nyewood Lane, Aldwick, Bognor Regis, West Sussex, PO21 2QB

T:	+44 (0) 1243 826880
E:	swanhse@globalnet.co.uk
W:	users.globalnet.co.uk/~swanhse
Bedrooms:	7 • £50.00-£70.00 per double room per night, breakfast included
Open:	Year round except Christmas and New Year
Description:	The warm and friendly Swan Guesthouse is situated in a prime position just 100 yards from the seafront.
Facilities:	⅟P🖵🍴
To Beach:	0.74 miles

BOGNOR REGIS – EAST OF THE PIER

White Horses ♦♦♦♦Guest Accommodation

Clyde Road, Felpham, Bognor Regis, West Sussex, PO22 7AH

T:	+44 (0) 1243 824320
E:	info@whitehorsesfelpham.co.uk
W:	whitehorsesfelpham.co.uk
Bedrooms:	6 • £60.00-£75.00 per double room per night, breakfast included
Open:	Seasonal opening – call for details
Description:	White Horses B&B is located in a quiet cul-de-sac just seconds from the sea and Felpham beach. A modernised, flint and brick house offering contemporary accommodation with on-site parking.
Facilities:	⅟P🖵🍴
To Beach:	0.71 miles

BOGNOR REGIS – EAST OF THE PIER

Willow Rise ♦♦♦♦Guest Accommodation

131 North Bersted Street, Bognor Regis, West Sussex, PO22 9AG

T:	+44 (0) 1243 829544
E:	gillboon@aol.com
W:	visitsussex.org
Bedrooms:	3 • £60.00-£70.00 per double room per night, breakfast included
Open:	Seasonal opening – call for details
Description:	A very comfortable 1930s house with panoramic views of the South Downs and Goodwood, on the outskirts of town, with excellent access to all amenities.
Facilities:	⅟P🖵🍴
To Beach:	1.65 miles

CLIMPING – LITTLEHAMPTON COASTGUARDS BEACH

Amberley Court ★★★★Guest Accommodation

Crookthorn Lane, Climping, near Littlehampton, West Sussex, BN17 5SN

T: +44 (0) 1903 725131
E: Msimmonds06@aol.com
W: visitsussex.org

Bedrooms: 6 • £70.00 per double room per night, breakfast included

Open: Year round except Christmas and New Year

Description: If a quiet break is required, with a lovely breakfast, in a wonderful part of Sussex – then book with Amberley Court. Owners will do all they can to make your stay special.

Facilities:

To Beach: 1.58 miles

LITTLEHAMPTON – COASTGUARDS BEACH

Arun Sands ★★★Guest Accommodation

84 South Terrace, Littlehampton, West Sussex, BN17 5LJ

T: +44 (0) 1903 732489
E: info@arun-sands.co.uk
W: arun-sands.co.uk

Bedrooms: 8 • £60.00 per double room per night, breakfast included • Debit/credit card accepted

Open: Year round except Christmas and New Year

Description: Arun Sands is a Victorian-style townhouse overlooking the seafront and greens, just 10 minutes' walk from the town centre.

Facilities:

To Beach: 0.26 miles

RUSTINGTON – LITTLEHAMPTON COASTGUARDS BEACH

The Kenmore ♦♦♦♦Guest Accommodation

Claigmar Road, Rustington, Littlehampton, BN16 2NL SILVER AWARD

T: +44 (0) 1903 784634
E: thekenmore@amserve.net
W: kenmoreguesthouse.co.uk

Bedrooms: 8 • £60.00 per double room per night, breakfast included • Debit/credit card accepted

Open: Year round except Christmas and New Year

Description: The Kenmore is a secluded Edwardian house in a quiet garden setting, in the heart of Rustington and close to the sea.

Facilities:

To Beach: 1.31 miles

WEST WITTERING

Wicks Farm Holiday Park

★★★★★Holiday & Camping Park

Redlands Lane, West Wittering, Chichester, PO20 8QE

T:	+44 (0) 1243 513116
E:	wicks.farm@virgin.net
W:	wicksfarm.co.uk
Pitches:	40 • £10.00-£15.50 per pitch, 2 people per night • Debit/credit card accepted
Open:	Year round
Description:	Peaceful, rural park six miles from Chichester. Ideal for families, close to sandy beach. Tennis court and shop. Dogs on leads accepted. Special rates for walkers.
Facilities:	[illegible]
To Beach:	1.87 miles

WICK – LITTLEHAMPTON COASTGUARDS

Sandfield House

♦♦♦♦Guest Accommodation

Lyminster Road, Wick, Littlehampton, BN17 7PG

T:	+44 (0) 1903 724129
E:	francesfarrerbrown@btconnect.com
W:	visitsussex.org
Bedrooms:	3 • £50.00-£75.00 per double room per night, breakfast included
Open:	Seasonal opening – call for details
Description:	A detached, Victorian family house set in two acres of grounds. Friendly welcome from professional family.
Facilities:	[illegible]
To Beach:	1.61 miles

WORTHING – WORTHING TOWN BEACH

Blair House Hotel

♦♦♦♦Guest Accommodation

11 St Georges Road, Worthing, BN11 2DS

T:	+44 (0) 1903 234071
E:	stay@blairhousehotel.co.uk
W:	blairhousehotel.co.uk
Bedrooms:	14 • £26.00-£30.00 per double room per night, room only • Debit/credit card accepted
Open:	Year round
Description:	Under the personal supervision of the proprietor, close to town centre and amenities, two minutes from the sea and bowling green. Secure parking.
Facilities:	[illegible]
To Beach:	0.5 miles

WORTHING – WORTHING TOWN BEACH

Edwardian Dreams ★★★★Guest Accommodation
77 Manor Road, Worthing, BN11 4SL SILVER AWARD

T:	+44 (0) 1903 218565
E:	info@edwardiandreams.co.uk
W:	edwardiandreams.co.uk
Bedrooms:	5 • £66.00 per double room per night, breakfast included • Debit/credit card accepted
Open:	Year round except Christmas and New Year
Description:	This 1903 Edwardian residence with five spacious, double rooms all en suite, is conveniently located close to town centre, beach, station and buses.
Facilities:	[symbols]
To Beach:	0.71 miles

WORTHING – WORTHING TOWN BEACH

Heenefields ★★★★Guest Accommodation
98 Heene Road, Worthing, BN11 3RE

T:	+44 (0) 1903 538780
E:	heenefields.guesthouse@virgin.net
W:	heenefields.com
Bedrooms:	16 • £26.00-£28.00 per double room per night, room only • Debit/credit card accepted
Open:	Year round
Description:	Heenefields is a Victorian house with character, located on the west side of the town centre, three minutes from the seafront.
Facilities:	[symbols]
To Beach:	0.67 miles

WORTHING – WORTHING TOWN BEACH

Woodlands Guesthouse ★★★★Guest Accommodation
20 Warwick Gardens, Worthing, BN11 1PF SILVER AWARD

T:	+44 (0) 1903 233557
E:	woodlands@sunnyworthing.fsnet.co.uk
W:	woodlandsworthing.com
Bedrooms:	10 • £26.00-£30.00 per double room per night, room only • Debit/credit card accepted
Open:	Year round
Description:	Family-run guesthouse providing home-cooked food and friendly service. All bedrooms well appointed and comfortably furnished. Off-street parking.
Facilities:	[symbols]
To Beach:	0.32 miles

SOUTH SHIELDS – SANDHAVEN BEACH

Best Western Sea Hotel ★★★Hotel

Sea Road, South Shields, NE33 2LD

T:	+44 (0) 1914 270999
E:	sea@bestwestern.co.uk
W:	seahotel.co.uk
Bedrooms:	37 • £67.00-£75.00 per double room per night, breakfast included • Debit/credit card; cheques/cash accepted
Open:	Year round
Description:	In the heart of Catherine Cookson country. Busy restaurant offering English, Continental and vegetarian cooking.
Facilities:	[symbols]
To Beach:	0.08 miles

SOUTH SHIELDS – SANDHAVEN BEACH

Forest Guesthouse ★★★★Guesthouse

117 Ocean Road, South Shields, NE33 2JL

T:	+44 (0) 1914 548160
E:	enquiries@forestguesthouse.com
W:	forestguesthouse.com
Bedrooms:	6 • £45.00-£50.00 per double room per night, breakfast included • Debit/credit card; cheques/cash accepted
Open:	Seasonal opening – call for details
Description:	Small, friendly, relaxed atmosphere. Rooms have video or DVD, Sky and Freeview. Central heating, showers in all rooms. En suite available. Tea-/coffee-making facilities. Playstation available. Video library. Fridges. Hairdryers and shavers.
Facilities:	[symbols]
To Beach:	0.4 miles

SOUTH SHIELDS – SANDHAVEN BEACH

Little Haven Hotel ★★★Hotel

River Drive, Little Haven, South Shields, NE33 1LH

T:	+44 (0) 1914 554455
E:	info@littlehavenhotel.com
W:	littlehavenhotel.com
Bedrooms:	62 • £62.00-£77.00 per double room per night, breakfast included • Debit/credit card accepted
Open:	Year round
Description:	Uniquely situated at the gateway of the river Tyne, the Little Haven Hotel boasts extensive views of the busy river, and Littlehaven Beach. Yet it is within 15 minutes of both Newcastle and Sunderland.
Facilities:	[symbols]
To Beach:	0.63 miles

SUNDERLAND – ROKER BEACH

Anchor Lodge Guesthouse ♦♦♦Guest Accommodation

16 Roker Terrace, Sunderland, SR6 9NB

T: +44 (0) 1915 674154
E: anchorlodge@btconnect.com
W: anchorlodgeonline.co.uk

Bedrooms: 8 • £42.00 per double room per night, breakfast included • Debit/credit card accepted

Open: Year round except Christmas and New Year

Description: Whether visiting family or friends, motoring, biking or sightseeing – make this your stop-off point. If you are seeking a special break give them a call. Private parking. Sea views and fabulous food for breakfast.

Facilities:

To Beach: 0.15 miles

SUNDERLAND – ROKER BEACH

Areldee Guesthouse ♦♦♦Guest Accommodation

18 Roker Terrace, Sunderland, SR6 9NB

T: +44 (0) 1915 141971
E: peter@areldeeguesthouse.freeserve.co.uk
W: abbeyandareldeeguesthouses.co.uk

Bedrooms: 15 • £42.00-£48.00 per double room per night, breakfast included • Debit/credit card; cheques/cash accepted

Open: Year round

Description: Family-run guesthouse on the seafront. Newly furnished en suite rooms with fabulous beach views. Breakfast may be served in your room.

Facilities:

To Beach: 0.24 miles

TYNEMOUTH – KING EDWARDS BAY

Martineau Guesthouse ★★★★Guesthouse

57 Front Street, Tynemouth, North Shields, NE30 4BX SILVER AWARD

T: +44 (0) 1912 960746
E: martineau.house@ukgateway.net
W: martineau-house.co.uk

Bedrooms: 3 • £70.00 per double room per night, breakfast included

Open: Year round

Description: Britain's first known lady political journalist, Harriet Martineau, convalesced here in 1840-1845. She was visited by Charlotte Brontë during this period. There is a plaque on the building dedicated to Ms Martineau.

Facilities:

To Beach: 0.27 miles

WHITLEY BAY – CULLERCOATS BAY BEACH

Avalon Hotel ★★★Guest Accommodation

26-28 South Parade, Whitley Bay, NE26 2RG

T:	+44 (0) 1912 510080
E:	info@theavalon.co.uk
W:	theavalon.co.uk
Bedrooms:	14 • £55.00 per double room per night, breakfast included • Debit/credit card; cheques/cash accepted
Open:	Year round
Description:	Small, friendly and comfortable, family-run hotel situated in the heart of Whitley Bay. Easy access to Northumberland.
Facilities:	
To Beach:	1.09 miles

WHITLEY BAY – CULLERCOATS BAY BEACH

Lindsay Guesthouse ★★★★Guesthouse

50 Victoria Avenue, Whitley Bay, NE26 2BA

T:	+44 (0) 1912 527341
E:	info@lindsayguesthouse.co.uk
W:	lindsayguesthouse.co.uk
Bedrooms:	4 • £60.00-£80.00 per double room per night, breakfast included • Debit/credit card; cheques/cash accepted
Open:	Year round
Description:	Small, family-run guesthouse offering quality en suite accommodation, close to the sea, town, transport system and all amenities.
Facilities:	
To Beach:	0.98 miles

WHITLEY BAY – CULLERCOATS BAY BEACH

Marlborough Hotel ★★★★Guest Accommodation

20-21 East Parade, The Promenade, Whitley Bay, NE26 1AP

T:	+44 (0) 1912 513628
E:	reception@marlborough-hotel.com
W:	marlborough-hotel.com
Bedrooms:	16 • £50.00-£70.00 per double room per night, breakfast included • Debit/credit card; cheques/cash accepted
Open:	Year round except Christmas and New Year
Description:	Traditional seaside hotel in the centre of the promenade with fine sea views. Individually-styled bedrooms.
Facilities:	
To Beach:	1.25 miles

WHITLEY BAY – CULLERCOATS BAY BEACH

Park Lodge Hotel ♦♦♦♦Guest Accommodation

162-164 Park Avenue, Whitley Bay, NE26 1AU

T:	+44 (0) 1912 526879
E:	parklodgehotel@hotmail.com
W:	parklodge-hotel.co.uk
Bedrooms:	14 • £70.00-£80.00 per double room per night, breakfast included • Debit/credit card; cheques/cash accepted
Open:	Seasonal opening – call for details
Description:	Small and friendly hotel in a good position near the beach and entertainments. Ideal position for touring historic Northumbria.
Facilities:	
To Beach:	1.3 miles

WHITLEY BAY – CULLERCOATS BAY BEACH

Rex Hotel ★★★Hotel

The Promenade, Whitley Bay, NE26 2RL

T:	+44 (0) 1912 523201
E:	reception@rex-hotel.com
W:	rex-hotel.com
Bedrooms:	69 • £75.00 per double room per night, breakfast included • Debit/credit card; cheques/cash accepted
Open:	Seasonal opening – call for details
Description:	Situated on the promenade with magnificent sea views. Excellent restaurant and friendly service, public bars and private residents' lounge. Private car park.
Facilities:	
To Beach:	1.11 miles

WHITLEY BAY – CULLERCOATS BAY BEACH

The Glen Esk Guesthouse ★★★Guesthouse

8 South Parade, Whitley Bay, NE26 2RG

T:	+44 (0) 1912 530103
E:	info@glenesk-guesthouse.co.uk
W:	glenesk-guesthouse.co.uk
Bedrooms:	11 • £40.00-£60.00 per twin room per night, breakfast included • Cheques/cash accepted
Open:	Seasonal opening – call for details
Description:	Centrally located for pubs, clubs and restaurants the rooms have satellite TV, tea-/coffee-making facilities, showers. Stag, hen and commercial guests welcome.
Facilities:	P
To Beach:	1.09 miles

WHITLEY BAY – CULLERCOATS BAY BEACH

York House Hotel ★★★★Guest Accommodation

106-110 Park Avenue, Whitley Bay, NE26 1DN

T:	+44 (0) 1912 528313
E:	reservations@yorkhousehotel.com
W:	yorkhousehotel.com
Bedrooms:	14 • £55.00-£70.00 per double room per night, breakfast included • Debit/credit card; cheques/cash accepted
Open:	Year round
Description:	Conveniently and centrally located. Well equipped bedrooms with en suite facilities. Additional benefit of fridges and microwaves in all rooms.
Facilities:	
To Beach:	1.23 miles

BRIDLINGTON – NORTH BEACH

Balmoral House ★★★★Guest Accommodation

21 Marshall Avenue, Bridlington, YO15 2DT

T:	+44 (0) 1262 676678
E:	brian@balmoral-house.com
W:	balmoral-house.com
Bedrooms:	9 • £52.00-£60.00 per double room per night, breakfast included
Open:	Year round
Description:	Small, privately-owned hotel, owner-managed, providing high quality accommodation, service and food in a non-smoking environment.
Facilities:	
To Beach:	0.78 miles

BRIDLINGTON – NORTH BEACH

Bay Court Hotel ★★★★Guest Accommodation

35a Sands Lane, Bridlington, YO15 2JG

T:	+44 (0) 1262 676288
E:	bay.court@virgin.net
W:	baycourt.co.uk
Bedrooms:	7 • £52.00-£64.00 per double room per night, breakfast included • Debit/credit card accepted
Open:	Seasonal opening – call for details
Description:	Bay Court Hotel offers sea views, relaxation, comfort and a high level of personal service will all help to make your stay a memorable and enjoyable one.
Facilities:	
To Beach:	0.25 miles

BRIDLINGTON – NORTH BEACH

Bluebell Guesthouse ♦♦♦Guest Accommodation

3 St Annes Road, Bridlington, YO15 2JB

T:	+44 (0) 1262 675163
E:	pam@mybluebell.net
W:	mybluebell.com
Bedrooms:	7 • £50.00 per double room per night, breakfast included
Open:	Seasonal opening – call for details
Description:	Providing high quality, no smoking accommodation. A child-free environment and excellent customer service. We make your comfort our business.
Facilities:	
To Beach:	0.26 miles

BRIDLINGTON – NORTH BEACH

Expanse Hotel ★★★Hotel

North Marine Drive, Bridlington, YO15 2LS

T:	+44 (0) 1262 675347
E:	reservations@expanse.co.uk
W:	expanse.co.uk
Bedrooms:	12 • £76.00-£132.00 per double room per night, breakfast included
Open:	Year round
Description:	In a unique position overlooking the beach and sea with panoramic views of the bay and of Flamborough Head.
Facilities:	
To Beach:	0.02 miles

BRIDLINGTON – NORTH BEACH

Maryland B&B ♦♦♦♦Guest Accommodation

66 Wellington Road, Bridlington, YO15 2AZ

T:	+44 (0) 1262 671088
E:	ann@maryland.me.uk
W:	maryland.me.uk
Bedrooms:	4 • £36.00-£46.00 per double room per night, breakfast included
Open:	Seasonal opening – call for details
Description:	Maryland is a family-run B&B offering welcoming, comfortable accommodation not far from the centre of Bridlington and its award-winning beaches. It has been given four diamond status for the quality of service and excellent guest care.
Facilities:	
To Beach:	0.64 miles

BRIDLINGTON – NORTH BEACH

Rags Restaurant & Hotel ♦♦♦♦Guest Accommodation

South Pier, East Riding of Yorkshire, YO15 3AN

T:	+44 (0) 1262 400355
E:	ragshotel@tesco.net
W:	ragshotel.co.uk
Bedrooms:	7 • £49.50-£80.00 per double room per night, breakfast included
Open:	Year round
Description:	A first-floor, harbour-view restaurant with ground-floor bistro/bar and seven very comfortable rooms. All have en suite facilities. Building used to be a RAF hanger in the war. It was said to be where Lawrence of Arabia hid.
Facilities:	
To Beach:	0.92 miles

BRIDLINGTON – NORTH BEACH

Victoria Hotel ♦♦♦Guest Accommodation

25/27 Victoria Road, Bridlington, YO15 2AT

T:	+44 (0) 1262 673871
E:	victoria.hotel@virgin.net
W:	victoriahotelbridlington.co.uk
Bedrooms:	7 • £45.00-£53.00 per double room per night, breakfast included • Debit/credit card accepted
Open:	Seasonal opening – call for details
Description:	Enjoy the special, friendly atmosphere of this well-established and very comfortable, family-run hotel. As soon as you arrive you can relax, safe in the knowledge that they will do everything possible to ensure you have a happy, carefree stay.
Facilities:	
To Beach:	0.76 miles

BRIDLINGTON – SOUTH BEACH

Seacourt Hotel ♦♦♦♦Guest Accommodation

76 South Marine Drive, Bridlington, YO15 3NS SILVER AWARD

T:	+44 (0) 1262 400872
E:	seacourt.hotel@tiscali.co.uk
W:	seacourt-hotel.co.uk
Bedrooms:	11 • £60.00-£80.00 per double room per night, breakfast included
Open:	Year round
Description:	The Seacourt Hotel stands quietly in a prime position overlooking the beautiful south bay with panoramic sea views.
Facilities:	
To Beach:	0.71 miles

BRIDLINGTON – SOUTH BEACH

Strathmore Hotel ★★★Guest Accommodation

63-65 Horsforth Avenue, Bridlington, YO15 3DH

T: +44 (0) 1262 602828
E: Strathmore_Hotel@Bridlington-EY.freeserve.co.uk
W: bridlington-ey.freeserve.co.uk

Bedrooms: 20 • £49.90 per double room per night, breakfast included

Open: Year round

Description: Family-run, licensed hotel 100 yards from the south beach. Entrance ramp, ground floor bedrooms. Disabled and handicapped welcome. Coaches welcome.

Facilities:

To Beach: 0.89 miles

BRIDLINGTON – SOUTH BEACH

The Bay Ridge Hotel ♦♦♦Guest Accommodation

11-13 Summerfield Road, Bridlington, YO15 3LF

T: +44 (0) 1262 673425
E: bayridgehotel@aol.com
W: bayridgehotel.co.uk

Bedrooms: 9 • £49.00-£50.00 per double room per night, breakfast included

Open: Year round

Description: The Bay Ridge is a family-run hotel, offering comfortable accommodation, a warm welcome, good home cooking and a friendly atmosphere.

Facilities: P

To Beach: 0.86 miles

BRIDLINGTON – SOUTH BEACH

The Jasmine Guesthouse ★★★Guesthouse

27-29 Richmond Street, Bridlington, YO15 3DL

T: +44 (0) 1262 676608
E: jasmineguesthouse@btinternet.com.
W: jasmineguesthouse.com

Bedrooms: 9 • £46.00-£48.00 per double room per night, breakfast included

Open: Year round

Description: Welcoming seaside B&B, licensed bar, minutes from seafront, harbour and shops. TV and hospitality trays in all rooms.

Facilities: TV

To Beach: 0.98 miles

CARNABY – SOUTH BEACH

Manor Court Hotel & Restaurant ★★★Hotel

53 Main Street, Carnaby, Bridlington, YO16 4UJ

T:	+44 (0) 1262 606468
E:	info@manorcourt.co.uk
W:	manorcourt.co.uk
Bedrooms:	13 • £75.00-£90.00 per double room per night, breakfast included
Open:	Seasonal opening – call for details
Description:	The hotel is approximately 2.5 miles from Bridlington. Awarded for the conversion from an 18thC farmhouse.
Facilities:	[symbols]
To Beach:	1.66 miles

FLAMBOROUGH – SOUTH LANDING

Thornwick & Sea Farm Holiday Centre

★★★★Holiday, Touring & Camping Park

North Marine Road, Flamborough, Bridlington, YO15 1AU ROSE AWARD

T:	+44 (0) 1262 850369
E:	enquiries@thornwickbay.co.uk
W:	thornwickbay.co.uk
Pitches:	350 • £12.50-£17.00 per caravan per night • Debit/credit card accepted
Open:	Seasonal opening – call for details
Description:	Large caravan park on the Heritage Coast with outstanding sea views and extensive walks. Offering something for all the family.
Facilities:	P [symbols]
To Beach:	1.5 miles

HORNSEA

Earlham House Guesthouse ★★★★B&B

59A Eastgate, Hornsea, HU18 1NB SILVER AWARD

T:	+44 (0) 1964 537809
E:	info@earlhamhouse.com
W:	earlhamhouse.com
Bedrooms:	3 • £60.00-£70.00 per double room per night, breakfast included • Debit/credit card accepted
Open:	Seasonal opening – call for details
Description:	A completely refurbished Edwardian house offering high quality accommodation, which opened in March 2006. Adjacent to Hornsea's award-winning promenade.
Facilities:	[symbols]
To Beach:	0.27 miles

SEWERBY – BRIDLINGTON, NORTH BEACH

Field House Farm Cottages ★★★★/★Self Catering

Jewison Lane, Sewerby, Bridlington, YO16 6YG

T:	+44 (0) 1262 674932
E:	john.foster@farmline.com
W:	fieldhousefarmcottages.co.uk
Units:	7 • £300.00-£650.00 per unit per week
Open:	Year round
Description:	Seven lovely cottages set amid a working farm. Discerning guests can stay in comfortable cottages close to the spectacular coast of Flamborough Head. New courtyard area is a sun-trap.
Facilities:	PUX
To Beach:	1.71 miles

SKIPSEA

Skirlington Leisure Park

★★★★★Holiday, Touring & Camping Park

Hornsea Road, Skipsea, Driffield, YO25 8SY — ROSE AWARD

T:	+44 (0) 1262 468213
E:	enquiries@skirlington.com
W:	skirlington.com
Pitches:	841 • £15.00-£20.00 per caravan per night
Open:	Seasonal opening – call for details
Description:	Skirlington Leisure Park is situated on the cliff top in open countryside, and has modern facilities. A family-run business with a reputation for high standards.
Facilities:	WP PUX
To Beach:	1 mile

WILSTHORPE

South Cliff Caravan Park

★★★★Holiday, Touring & Camping Park

Wilsthorpe, Bridlington, YO15 3QN

T:	+44 (0) 1262 671051
E:	southcliff@eastriding.gov.uk
W:	southcliff.co.uk
Pitches:	369 • £15.00 per pitch, 2 people per night • Debit/credit card accepted
Open:	Seasonal opening – call for details
Description:	South Cliff Caravan Park is 300 yards from clean, safe, sandy beaches, one mile south of Bridlington. Bus service to town, also a shop, takeaway and leisure complex including bars, children's lounge and restaurant.
Facilities:	PX
To Beach:	0.29 miles

CAYTON – CAYTON BAY BEACH

Killerby Cottage Farm ★★★★Guest Accommodation

Killerby Lane, Cayton, Scarborough, YO11 3NN SILVER AWARD

T:	+44 (0) 1723 581236
E:	val@stained-glass.demon.co.uk
W:	smoothhound.co.uk/hotels/killerby
Bedrooms:	3 • £70.00-£90.00 per double room per night, breakfast included • Debit/credit card accepted
Open:	Seasonal opening – call for details
Description:	Killerby Cottage Farm is in the countryside between Scarborough and Filey. Tastefully decorated, good food, lovely garden.
Facilities:	
To Beach:	1.11 miles

CAYTON BAY

Cayton Village Caravan Park

★★★★★Camping & Touring Park

Mill Lane, Cayton Bay, Scarborough, YO11 3NN

T:	+44 (0) 1723 583171
E:	info@caytontouring.co.uk
W:	caytontouring.co.uk
Pitches:	325 • £11.50-£22.00 per caravan per night • Debit/credit card accepted
Open:	Year round
Description:	Quiet, sheltered touring and tenting park adjoining Cayton village church. Half-a-mile to Cayton Bay Beach, three miles south of Scarborough, four miles to Filey.
Facilities:	P
To Beach:	0.76 miles

DUNSLEY – SANDSEND BEACH

Dunsley Hall Country House Hotel ★★★Hotel

Dunsley, Whitby, YO21 3TL SILVER AWARD

T:	+44 (0) 1947 893437
E:	reception@dunsleyhall.com
W:	dunsleyhall.com
Bedrooms:	19 • £140.00-£177.00 per double room per night, breakfast included • Debit/credit card accepted
Open:	Year round
Description:	Large country house in four acres of grounds. Extensive carved oak panelling. Indoor pool. Library, bar, lounge and bistro.
Facilities:	
To Beach:	1.08 miles

ELLERBY – RUNSWICK BAY

Ellerby Hotel

★★★★Inn
SILVER AWARD

Ryeland Lane, Ellerby, Saltburn-by-the-Sea, TS13 5LP

T:	+44 (0) 1947 840342
E:	david@ellerbyhotel.co.uk
W:	ellerbyhotel.co.uk
Bedrooms:	9 • £76.00 per double room per night, breakfast included
Open:	Year round
Description:	Ellerby Hotel is an inn owned and managed by the Alderson family since 1985. It is located in a beautiful country setting only eight miles from Whitby.
Facilities:	
To Beach:	0.96 miles

FILEY

Athol Guesthouse

♦♦♦♦Guest Accommodation

67 West Avenue, Filey, YO14 9AX

T:	+44 (0) 1723 515189
E:	atholhouse@tiscali.co.uk
W:	athol-guesthouse.co.uk
Bedrooms:	5 • £50.00-£52.00 per double room per night, breakfast included
Open:	Seasonal opening – call for details
Description:	An Edwardian semi-detached house on a tree-lined avenue. It is centrally located for all amenities, and five minutes from the seafront. It has five bedrooms, all en suite, two of which are family rooms. All are decorated to high standard.
Facilities:	
To Beach:	0.41 miles

FILEY

Filey Brigg Caravan & Country Park

★★★★Camping & Touring Park

Church Cliff Drive, North Cliff, Arndale, Filey, YO14 9ET

T:	+44 (0) 1723 513852
E:	fileybrigg@scarborough.gov.uk
W:	scarborough.gov.uk
Pitches:	162 • £8.50-£15.00 per motor caravan per night
Open:	Seasonal opening – call for details
Description:	Filey Brigg Caravan & Country Park is set in 70 acres of country park. Majestic views over Filey Bay coastline. Ideal for visiting the North York Moors.
Facilities:	P
To Beach:	0.26 miles

FILEY

The Forge

♦♦♦♦Guest Accommodation

23 Rutland Street, Filey, YO14 9JA

T:	+44 (0) 1723 512379
E:	theforge1@tiscali.co.uk
W:	smoothound.co.uk
Bedrooms:	4 • £50.00 per double room per night, breakfast included
Open:	Seasonal opening – call for details
Description:	The Forge Guesthouse is a small, friendly, family-run guesthouse found 40 yards from Crescent Gardens.
Facilities:	
To Beach:	0.36 miles

FILEY

White Lodge Hotel

★★★Hotel

The Crescent, Filey, YO14 9JX

T:	+44 (0) 1723 514771
E:	info@whitelodgehotelfiley.co.uk
W:	whitelodgehotelfiley.co.uk
Bedrooms:	19 • £96.00-£130.00 per double room per night, breakfast included • Debit/credit card accepted
Open:	Year round
Description:	Cliff top hotel overlooking the bay, close to the town centre and golf course. An ideal location for a relaxing holiday.
Facilities:	
To Beach:	0.5 miles

FYLINGTHORPE – ROBIN HOOD'S BAY

Middlewood Farm Holiday Park

★★★★★Holiday, Touring & Camping Park

Middlewood Lane, Fylingthorpe, Whitby, YO22 4UF ROSE AWARD

T:	+44 (0) 1947 880414
E:	info@middlewoodfarm.com
W:	middlewoodfarm.com
Pitches:	120 • £12.50-£18.00 per caravan per night • Debit/credit card accepted
Open:	Year round
Description:	Small peaceful park, delightfully situated. Ten minutes' walk over fields to beach, pub and Robin Hood's Bay. Magnificent country, sea and moorland views.
Facilities:	P
To Beach:	0.49 miles

LEBBERSTON – CAYTON BAY BEACH

Crows Nest Caravan Park ★★★★Holiday Park

Gristhorpe, Filey, YO14 9PS ROSE AWARD

T:	+44 (0) 1723 582206
E:	enquiries@crowsnestcaravanpark.com
W:	crowsnestcaravanpark.com
Pitches:	240 • £14.00-£20.00 per caravan per night
Open:	Seasonal opening – call for details
Description:	Family-owned park for families and couples only. Full range of facilities. Ideal centre for exploring Scarborough and Filey.
Facilities:	P
To Beach:	1.38 miles

LEBBERSTON – CAYTON BAY BEACH

Flower of May Holiday Parks

★★★★★Holiday, Touring & Camping Park

Lebberston, Scarborough, YO11 3NU ROSE AWARD

T:	+44 (0) 1723 584311
E:	info@flowerofmay.com
W:	flowerofmay.com
Pitches:	337 • £13.00-£17.50 per caravan per night
Open:	Seasonal opening – call for details
Description:	Family park near the top of cliffs, with marvellous views of the coastline and Yorkshire Wolds. Dogs accepted in tents and touring caravans, only at certain times of the year.
Facilities:	P
To Beach:	1.33 miles

LEBBERSTON – CAYTON BAY BEACH

Lebberston Touring Park ★★★★★Touring Park

Lebberston, Scarborough, YO11 3PE

T:	+44 (0) 1723 585723
E:	info@lebberstontouring.co.uk
W:	lebberstontouring.co.uk
Pitches:	125 • £11.50-£17.00 per caravan per night • Debit/credit card accepted
Open:	Seasonal opening – call for details
Description:	Gently sloping site with excellent views. Quiet country park suitable for maturer couples and young families.
Facilities:	P✕
To Beach:	1.44 miles

REDCAR – REDCAR LIFEBOAT BEACH

All Welcome In ★★Guest Accommodation

81 Queen Street, Redcar, TS10 1BG

T:	+44 (0) 1642 484790
E:	allwelcomein@yahoo.co.uk
W:	allwelcomein.co.uk
Bedrooms:	6 • £30.00-£40.00 per double room per night, breakfast included
Open:	Year round
Description:	Friendly-run guesthouse, clean, warm and good food. Central to all amenities, many extra facilities available. Good value!
Facilities:	[facility symbols]
To Beach:	0.31 miles

REDCAR – REDCAR LIFEBOAT BEACH

Springdale House ★★★★B&B

3 Nelson Terrace, Redcar, TS10 1RX

T:	+44 (0) 1642 297169
E:	reservations@springdalehouse.co.uk
W:	springdalehouse.co.uk
Bedrooms:	2 • £70.00 per double room per night, breakfast included
Open:	Seasonal opening – call for details
Description:	Beautiful Victorian building, recently renovated, offering two guest rooms both en suite, dining area and separate lounge with Sky TV.
Facilities:	[facility symbols] P
To Beach:	0.31 miles

ROBIN HOODS BAY

Marnardale Cottage ★★★★B&B

8 Sunny Side, Robin Hood's Bay, Whitby, YO22 4SR

T:	+44 (0) 1947 880677
W:	marnardalecottage.co.uk
Bedrooms:	2 • £55.00 per double room per night, breakfast included
Open:	Year round
Description:	Marnardale Cottage is in the old bay town at the end of Sunny Side next to its own land, 10 acres of beautiful countryside, yet is only 100 yards from the beach. A perfect place for walking the Cleveland Way.
Facilities:	[facility symbols] P
To Beach:	0.15 miles

RUNSWICK – RUNSWICK BAY

The Firs ★★★★Guesthouse

26 Hinderwell Lane, Runswick, Saltburn-by-the-Sea, TS13 5HR

T: +44 (0) 1947 840433
E: mandy.shackleton@talk21.com
W: the-firs.co.uk

Bedrooms: 12 • £65.00 per double room per night, breakfast included

Open: Seasonal opening – call for details

Description: Detached stone-built, spacious property situated at the picturesque coastal village of Runswick Bay. All rooms en suite, private parking.

Facilities:

To Beach: 0.5 miles

RUSWARP – WHITBY WEST CLIFF

Ruswarp Hall ♦♦♦Guest Accommodation

4-6 High Street, Ruswarp, Whitby, YO21 1NH

T: +44 (0) 1947 602801
E: da@ytb.org.uk
W: ruswarphall.co.uk

Bedrooms: 12 • £60.00-£74.00 per double room per night, breakfast included

Open: Seasonal opening – call for details

Description: A Listed Jacobean hall standing in its own grounds. It has a guest lounge, dining room and cosy bar boasting more than 100 malt whiskies. Afternoon teas served in the beautiful landscaped gardens.

Facilities:

To Beach: 1.45 miles

SALTBURN-BY-THE-SEA

Diamond Guesthouse ★★★★Guest Accommodation

9 Diamond Street, Saltburn-By-The-Sea, TS12 1EB

T: +44 (0) 1287 207049
E: diamondhouse9@ntlworld.com
W: diamondguesthouse.co.uk

Bedrooms: 3 • £30.00-£50.00 per double room per night, breakfast included

Open: Seasonal opening – call for details

Description: Family-run guesthouse in a picturesque Victorian seaside resort.

Facilities:

To Beach: 0.17 miles

SALTBURN-BY-THE-SEA

The Rose Garden ★★★★B&B

20 Hilda Place, Saltburn-By-The-Sea, TS12 1BP

T:	+44 (0) 1287 622947
E:	enquiries@therosegarden.co.uk
W:	therosegarden.co.uk
Bedrooms:	2 • £60.00 per double room per night, breakfast included
Open:	Seasonal opening – call for details
Description:	Large, Victorian, terraced house with small front garden. Well situated for all amenities in a charming seaside resort.
Facilities:	
To Beach:	0.4 miles

SALTBURN-BY-THE-SEA

Victorian Guesthouse ♦♦♦♦Guest Accommodation

1 Oxford Street, Saltburn-By-The-Sea, TS12 1LG

T:	+44 (0) 1287 625237
E:	susanmorgan4@ntlworld.com
W:	victorian-guesthouse.co.uk
Bedrooms:	2 • £50.00 per double room per night, breakfast included
Open:	Year round
Description:	A beautiful guesthouse in the heart of Saltburn. This friendly family-run establishment offers a relaxed and comfortable atmosphere.
Facilities:	P
To Beach:	0.5 miles

SCARBOROUGH – NORTH BAY

Clairmont Hotel ★Hotel

20 Ryndleside, Scarborough, YO12 6AD

T:	+44 (0) 1723 362288
E:	clairmonthotel@yahoo.co.uk
W:	clairmonthotel.co.uk
Bedrooms:	12 • £40.00-£56.00 per double room per night, breakfast included
Open:	Year round
Description:	Clairmont Hotel is in a scenic position overlooking Peasholm Park and The Glen, convenient for all the attractions of North Bay. All bedrooms are en suite.
Facilities:	P
To Beach:	0.5 miles

SCARBOROUGH – NORTH BAY

Delmont ★★Hotel

18-19 Blenheim Terrace, Scarborough, YO12 7HE

T: +44 (0) 1723 364500
E: delmonthotelscar@aol.com
W: mamut.com/delmonthotelscarboro

Bedrooms: 51 • £42.00-£74.00 per double room per night, breakfast included

Open: Year round

Description: Warm, friendly hotel with superb views over North Bay. Close to the town centre, beach and parks. Yorkshire breakfasts, choice of evening meals and live entertainment.

Facilities:

To Beach: 0.49 miles

SCARBOROUGH – NORTH BAY

Donnington Hotel ♦♦♦Guest Accommodation

13 Givendale Road, Scarborough, YO12 6LE

T: +44 (0) 1723 374394
E: bookings@donningtonhotel.co.uk
W: donningtonhotel.co.uk

Bedrooms: 5 • £50.00 per double room per night, breakfast included • Debit/credit card accepted

Open: Year round

Description: The Donnington is a small and friendly B&B that lies five minutes' walk from Scarborough's North Bay sandy beach and attractions, including Peasholm Park.

Facilities:

To Beach: 0.44 miles

SCARBOROUGH – NORTH BAY

Gordon Hotel ★★★★Guesthouse

Ryndleside, Scarborough, YO12 6AD

T: +44 (0) 1723 362177
E: sales@gordonhotel.co.uk
W: gordonhotel.co.uk

Bedrooms: 10 • £40.00-£50.00 per double room per night, breakfast included

Open: Year round

Description: Gordon Hotel is a friendly, family-run licensed hotel overlooking Peasholm Park. Family rooms are available. Senior citizen discount. TV, complementary tray, hairdryers and clock radios.

Facilities: TV

To Beach: 0.44 miles

SCARBOROUGH – NORTH BAY

Hotel Majestic ★★Hotel

57 Northstead Manor Drive, Scarborough, YO12 6AG

T:	+44 (0) 1723 363806
E:	ingrid@majestichotel.co.uk
W:	hotelmajestic.co.uk
Bedrooms:	20 • £46.00-£54.00 per double room per night, breakfast included
Open:	Seasonal opening – call for details
Description:	Modern, licensed hotel facing Peasholm Park, near the beach and pools. All rooms have en suite facilities. Private car park.
Facilities:	P
To Beach:	0.3 miles

SCARBOROUGH – NORTH BAY

Hotel Phoenix ★★★Guesthouse

8-9 Rutland Terrace, Queens Parade, Scarborough, YO12 7JB

T:	+44 (0) 1723 501150
E:	info@hotel-phoenix.co.uk
W:	hotel-phoenix.co.uk
Bedrooms:	14 • £50.00-£66.00 per double room per night, breakfast included • Debit/credit card accepted
Open:	Seasonal opening – call for details
Description:	Hotel Phoenix is a Victorian house overlooking Scarborough's north bay and only minutes' walk from the beach, the castle and many other local attractions.
Facilities:	P
To Beach:	0.5 miles

SCARBOROUGH – NORTH BAY

Howdale ♦♦♦♦Guest Accommodation

121 Queen's Parade, Scarborough, YO12 7HU

T:	+44 (0) 1723 372696
E:	admin@howdalehotel.co.uk
W:	howdalehotel.co.uk
Bedrooms:	15 • £48.00-£56.00 per double room per night, breakfast included • Debit/credit card accepted
Open:	Seasonal opening – call for details
Description:	Beautifully situated overlooking the North Bay and castle, yet close to town. Thirteen of the excellent bedrooms have en suite facilities, many have sea views. All are well equipped with TVs, hairdryers and clock-radios.
Facilities:	P TV
To Beach:	0.19 miles

SCARBOROUGH – NORTH BAY

Kenways Guesthouse ★★★Guesthouse

9 Victoria Park Avenue, Scarborough, YO12 7TR

T:	+44 (0) 1723 365757
E:	info@kenwaysguesthouse.co.uk
W:	kenwaysguesthouse.co.uk
Bedrooms:	7 • £40.00-£42.00 per double room per night, breakfast included
Open:	Seasonal opening – call for details
Description:	Kenways is a small, friendly, family-run guesthouse, close to North Bay amenities including bowls centre, cricket ground, Peasholm Park and Atlantis. Only five minutes' walk to the sea and beautiful views of North Bay.
Facilities:	
To Beach:	0.19 miles

SCARBOROUGH – NORTH BAY

Lincoln Hotel ★★★Guest Accommodation

112 Columbus Ravine, Scarborough, YO12 7QZ

T:	+44 (0) 1723 500897
E:	enquiries@lincolnhotel.net
W:	lincolnhotel.net
Bedrooms:	7 • £50.00-£80.00 per double room per night, breakfast included
Open:	Seasonal opening – call for details
Description:	Family-run, licensed hotel in a pleasant area. Private car park, all rooms offer en suite facilities, TV, tea-making facilities etc, children welcome, good food.
Facilities:	P TV
To Beach:	0.27 miles

SCARBOROUGH – NORTH BAY

Lyncris Manor Hotel ★★★★Guest Accommodation

45 Northstead Manor Drive, Scarborough, YO12 6AF

T:	+44 (0) 1723 361052
E:	lyncris@manorhotel.fsnet.co.uk
W:	manorhotel.fsnet.co.uk
Bedrooms:	6 • £36.00-£40.00 per double room per night, breakfast included
Open:	Seasonal opening – call for details
Description:	Small, friendly, detached, family-run licensed hotel in unrivalled position overlooking Peasholm Park and North Bay. High standards. Recommended in *Which?*
Facilities:	
To Beach:	0.33 miles

SCARBOROUGH – NORTH BAY

Norlands Hotel ♦♦♦♦Guest Accommodation

10 Weydale Avenue, Scarborough, YO12 6BA

T:	+44 (0) 1723 362606
E:	info@norlandshotel.co.uk
W:	norlandshotel.co.uk
Bedrooms:	9 • £38.00-£54.00 per double room per night, breakfast included
Open:	Seasonal opening – call for details
Description:	The well-established Norlands Hotel holds an outstanding position with panoramic views over the North Bay and Scarborough Castle.
Facilities:	
To Beach:	0.29 miles

SCARBOROUGH – NORTH BAY

Ryndle Court Private Hotel ★★Hotel

47 Northstead Manor Drive, Scarborough, YO12 6AF

T:	+44 (0) 1723 375188
E:	toni-shelton@hotmail.co.uk
W:	ryndlecourt.co.uk
Bedrooms:	14 • £68.00-£72.00 per double room per night, breakfast included • Debit/credit card accepted
Open:	Year round
Description:	Imposing, detached hotel, ideally situated overlooking Peasholm Park. Near to the sea and leisure parks.
Facilities:	
To Beach:	0.39 miles

SCARBOROUGH – NORTH BAY

Scalby Close Park ★★★★Holiday, Touring & Camping Park

Burniston Road, Scarborough, YO13 0DA — ROSE AWARD

T:	+44 (0) 1723 365908
E:	info@scalbyclose.co.uk
W:	scalbyclosepark.co.uk
Pitches:	97 • £10.00-£18.00 per caravan per night
Open:	Seasonal opening – call for details
Description:	Long established, well-maintained, landscaped, family-run site with all the latest facilities expected by today's campers (heated, modern shower block, waste and water super pitches etc). Accommodates tents, caravans and motor homes.
Facilities:	
To Beach:	1.42 miles

SCARBOROUGH – NORTH BAY

Sunningdale Hotel ★★★★Guesthouse

105 Peasholm Drive, Scarborough, YO12 7NB

T: +44 (0) 1723 372041
E: sunningdale@yorkshire.net
W: sunningdale-scarborough.co.uk

Bedrooms: 10 • £50.00 per double room per night, breakfast included • Debit/credit card accepted

Open: Seasonal opening – call for details

Description: The Sunningdale is a non-smoking, detached, family-run guesthouse, opposite Peasholm Park. All rooms are en suite, with cleanliness assured. Within easy walking distance of the beach and close to the North Yorkshire Moors.

Facilities:

To Beach: 0.25 miles

SCARBOROUGH – NORTH BAY

Sylvern Hotel ★★★★Guest Accommodation

25 New Queen Street, Scarborough, YO12 7HJ

T: +44 (0) 1723 360952
E: sylvernhotel@aol.com
W: smoothhound.co.uk/hotels/sylvern.html

Bedrooms: 8 • £48.00-£50.00 per double room per night, breakfast included

Open: Year round

Description: Family-run hotel ideally situated close to both bays and town centre. Children and pets welcome.

Facilities:

To Beach: 0.5 miles

SCARBOROUGH – NORTH BAY

The Alexander Hotel ★★★★Guest Accommodation

33 Burniston Road, Scarborough, YO12 6PG SILVER AWARD

T: +44 (0) 1723 363178
E: alex@atesto.freeserve.co.uk
W: alexanderhotelscarborough.co.uk

Bedrooms: 10 • £56.00-£64.00 per double room per night, breakfast included • Debit/credit card accepted

Open: Seasonal opening – call for details

Description: Detached hotel, five minutes from North Beach and Peasholm Park. For the discerning, near to golf course, non-smoking, excellent cuisine and car park.

Facilities:

To Beach: 0.34 miles

SCARBOROUGH – NORTH BAY

The Stuart House Hotel ★★★★Guest Accommodation

1 & 2 Rutland Terrace, Queens Parade, Scarborough, YO12 7JB

T: +44 (0) 1723 373768
E: h.graham@btconnect.com
W: thestuarthousehotel.com

Bedrooms: 13 • £50.00 per double room per night, breakfast included

Open: Year round

Description: Friendly, family-run hotel, superbly situated overlooking North Bay and beach. Within 10-minute walk of shopping centre.

Facilities:

To Beach: 0.5 miles

SCARBOROUGH – NORTH BAY

The Whiteley Hotel ♦♦♦♦Guest Accommodation

99-101 Queens Parade, Scarborough, YO12 7HY SILVER AWARD

T: +44 (0) 1723 373514
E: whiteleyhotel@bigfoot.com
W: yorkshirecoast.co.uk/whiteley

Bedrooms: 10 • £48.00-£52.00 per double room per night, breakfast included • Debit/credit card accepted

Open: Seasonal opening – call for details

Description: Small, family-run hotel is in an elevated position overlooking the North Bay and close to the town centre. Non-smoking.

Facilities:

To Beach: 0.3 miles

SCARBOROUGH – SOUTH BAY

Ashburton Hotel ♦♦♦Guest Accommodation

43 Valley Road, Scarborough, YO11 2LX

T: +44 (0) 1723 374382
E: stay@ashburtonhotel.co.uk
W: ashburtonhotel.co.uk

Bedrooms: 8 • £40.00-£45.00 per double room per night, breakfast included • Debit/credit card accepted

Open: Year round

Description: The Ashburton Hotel aims to offer the combination of first class business and holiday accommodation combined with great value and a friendly, relaxed atmosphere.

Facilities: P

To Beach: 0.46 miles

SCARBOROUGH – SOUTH BAY

Brambles Lodge ★★★Guest Accommodation

156-158 Filey Road, Scarborough, YO11 3AA

T: +44 (0) 1723 374613
E: nightingales22@aol.com
W: accommodation.uk.net/brambleslodge.htm

Bedrooms: 7 • £46.00-£50.00 per double room per night, breakfast included

Open: Seasonal opening – call for details

Description: Free wireless, internet access, all en suite and non-smoking, ample private parking, very dog friendly and children welcome (6-14 years).

Facilities:

To Beach: 1.05 miles

SCARBOROUGH – SOUTH BAY

Cavendish Hotel ★★★★Guest Accommodation

53 Esplanade Road, Scarborough, YO11 2AT

T: +44 (0) 1723 362108
E: anne@cavendishscarborough.co.uk
W: cavendishscarborough.co.uk

Bedrooms: 3 • £56.00-£60.00 per double room per night, breakfast included

Open: Year round

Description: Small, family-run hotel, offering excellent home cooking, close to many amenities.

Facilities:

To Beach: 0.24 miles

SCARBOROUGH – SOUTH BAY

Esplanade Gardens Guesthouse ★★★Guest Accommodation

24 Esplanade Gardens, Scarborough, YO11 2AP

T: +44 (0) 1723 360728
E: kerry@khubbard.fsnet.co.uk
W: esplanadegardensscarborough.co.uk

Bedrooms: 10 • £40.00-£50.00 per double room per night, breakfast included • Debit/credit card accepted

Open: Seasonal opening – call for details

Description: This is a small, family-run guesthouse offering clean and comfortable accommodation with a friendly welcome and excellent service.

Facilities:

To Beach: 0.2 miles

SCARBOROUGH – SOUTH BAY

Mansion House Hotel ♦♦♦♦Guest Accommodation

45 Esplanade, South Cliff, Scarborough, YO11 2AY

T:	+44 (0) 1723 373930
E:	mansionhouse45@aol.com
W:	mansionhousehotel.com
Bedrooms:	18 • £86.00-£108.00 per double room per night, breakfast included • Debit/credit card accepted
Open:	Year round
Description:	Very comfortable, private, licensed hotel, overlooking the South Bay. Close to the Spa complex and cliff lift.
Facilities:	
To Beach:	0.18 miles

SCARBOROUGH – SOUTH BAY

Moseley Lodge Hotel ♦♦♦♦Guest Accommodation

26 Avenue Victoria, South Cliff, Scarborough, YO11 2QT

T:	+44 (0) 1723 360564
E:	holidays@moseleylodge.co.uk
W:	moseleylodge.co.uk
Bedrooms:	9 • £48.00 per double room per night, breakfast included • Debit/credit card accepted
Open:	Seasonal opening – call for details
Description:	Moseley Lodge is an elegant, Victorian hotel close to spa conference centre. Italian and Rose Gardens and cliff lift to beach. Most rooms have en suite facilities. The facilities in each room includes hospitality trays.
Facilities:	
To Beach:	0.26 miles

SCARBOROUGH – SOUTH BAY

Mount House Hotel ♦♦♦♦Guest Accommodation

33 Trinity Road, South Cliff, Scarborough, YO11 2TD

T:	+44 (0) 1723 362967
E:	bookings@mounthouse-hotel.co.uk
W:	mounthouse-hotel.co.uk
Bedrooms:	8 • £48.00-£56.00 per double room per night, breakfast included
Open:	Seasonal opening – call for details
Description:	Victorian hotel on a quiet road, 10 minutes' walk to the cliff lift, giving access to the Spa and south beach. Traditional home cooking.
Facilities:	
To Beach:	0.5 miles

SCARBOROUGH – SOUTH BAY

New Southlands Hotel ♦♦♦Guest Accommodation

West Street, Scarborough, YO11 2QW

T:	+44 (0) 1803 290029
E:	reservations@shearingsholidays.co.uk
W:	shearingsholidays.com
Bedrooms:	56 • £30.00-£45.00 per double room per night, breakfast included
Open:	Year round
Description:	Just off the South Cliff close to beach and town centre. Elegant and spacious public areas. Entertainment every night.
Facilities:	
To Beach:	0.19 miles

SCARBOROUGH – SOUTH BAY

Powys Lodge Hotel ♦♦♦♦Guest Accommodation

2 Westbourne Road, South Cliff, Scarborough, YO11 2SP

T:	+44 (0) 1723 374019
E:	info@powyslodge.co.uk
W:	powyslodge.co.uk
Bedrooms:	9 • £52.00-£60.00 per double room per night, breakfast included • Debit/credit card accepted
Open:	Seasonal opening – call for details
Description:	Small, family-run, licensed hotel convenient for the Spa, South Beach and the town. Colour TV lounge, cocktail bar and pleasant dining room. Pool table. All rooms offer en suite facilities and are centrally heated.
Facilities:	
To Beach:	0.45 miles

SCARBOROUGH – SOUTH BAY

Princess Court Guesthouse

★★★★Guest Accommodation

11 Princess Royal Terrace, Scarborough, YO11 2RP

T:	+44 (0) 1723 501922
E:	iruin@princesscourt.co.uk
W:	princesscourt.co.uk
Bedrooms:	7 • £50.00-£70.00 per double room per night, breakfast included
Open:	Seasonal opening – call for details
Description:	Princess Court is a family-run guesthouse on the South Cliff area of Scarborough, near to the Esplanade, Italian Gardens and Spa Complex. All seven of its spotless rooms have en suite facilities.
Facilities:	
To Beach:	0.33 miles

SCARBOROUGH – SOUTH BAY

Redcliffe Hotel ★★★★Guest Accommodation

18 Prince of Wales Terrace, South Bay, Scarborough, YO11 2AL

T:	+44 (0) 1723 372310
E:	da@ytb.org.uk
W:	theredcliffehotel.com
Bedrooms:	11 • £48.00-£76.00 per double room per night, breakfast included
Open:	Year round
Description:	Delightful, Victorian house totally refurbished and sympathetically restored, now providing 11 lovely rooms with every facility. A true home from home.
Facilities:	
To Beach:	0.15 miles

SCARBOROUGH – SOUTH BAY

Red Lea Hotel ★★Hotel

Prince of Wales Terrace, Scarborough, YO11 2AJ

T:	+44 (0) 1723 362431
E:	redlea@globalnet.co.uk
W:	redleahotel.co.uk
Bedrooms:	69 • £56.00-£78.00 per double room per night, breakfast included • Debit/credit card accepted
Open:	Year round
Description:	Elegant, period property with views from the South Cliff to the sea. Ideally placed for conference centre and all amenities.
Facilities:	
To Beach:	0.08 miles

SCARBOROUGH – SOUTH BAY

Riviera Hotel ♦♦♦♦Guest Accommodation

St Nicholas Cliff, Scarborough, YO11 2ES

T:	+44 (0) 1723 372277
E:	rivierahotel@scarborough.co.uk
W:	rivierahotel.scarborough.co.uk
Bedrooms:	21 • £56.00-£74.00 per double room per night, breakfast included
Open:	Seasonal opening – call for details
Description:	Ideal central position in luxurious surroundings only yards from the beach, Spa, and town centre. A happy holiday is assured.
Facilities:	
To Beach:	0.48 miles

WHITBY – WEST CLIFF

Grove Hotel
♦♦♦♦Guest Accommodation

36 Bagdale, Whitby, YO21 1QL

T: +44 (0) 1947 603551
E: angelaswales@btconnect.com
W: smoothhound.co.uk/hotels/grove2.html

Bedrooms: 8 • £45.00-£50.00 per double room per night, breakfast included

Open: Seasonal opening – call for details

Description: Small, family-run guesthouse near to all amenities. Parking for each room. All rooms are en suite or have own private bathroom. Short distance from train and bus stations. Three-minute walk to harbour side and main shopping area.

Facilities:

To Beach: 0.5 miles

WHITBY – WEST CLIFF

Haven Crest
♦♦♦♦Guest Accommodation

137 Upgang Lane, Whitby, YO21 3JW SILVER AWARD

T: +44 (0) 1947 605187
E: enquiries@havencrest.co.uk
W: havencrest.co.uk

Bedrooms: 3 • £56.00-£68.00 per double room per night, breakfast included • Debit/credit card accepted

Open: Seasonal opening – call for details

Description: Haven Crest is a superior guesthouse for the discerning guest with warm, comfortable double rooms. All offer en suite facilities.

Facilities: P

To Beach: 0.5 miles

WHITBY – WEST CLIFF

High Tor
★★★★Guesthouse

7 Normanby Terrace, Whitby, YO21 3ES

T: +44 (0) 1947 602507
E: hightorguesthouse@hotmail.com
W: hightorguesthouse.co.uk

Bedrooms: 6 • £50.00-£60.00 per double room per night, breakfast included

Open: Year round

Description: Family-run guesthouse in the West Cliff area of the town. Emphasis on food and comfort. Refurbished rooms. Close to sea and town.

Facilities:

To Beach: 0.23 miles

WHITBY – WEST CLIFF

Sandfield House Farm Caravan Park

★★★★★Touring Park

Sandsend Road, Whitby, YO21 3SR

T:	+44 (0) 1947 602660
E:	info@sandfieldhousefarm.co.uk
W:	sandfieldhousefarm.co.uk
Pitches:	80 • £11.50-£14.00 per caravan per night
Open:	Seasonal opening – call for details
Description:	Good quality, clean, quiet park in lovely countryside. Close to long, sandy beach. One mile from Whitby centre.
Facilities:	P
To Beach:	0.88 miles

WHITBY – WEST CLIFF

Sandpiper Guesthouse

★★★★Guesthouse

4 Belle Vue Terrace, Whitby, YO21 3EY

T:	+44 (0) 1947 600246
E:	enquiries@sandpiperhouse.co.uk
W:	sandpiperhouse.co.uk
Bedrooms:	8 • £53.00 per double room per night, breakfast included
Open:	Seasonal opening – call for details
Description:	Comfortable, well-presented, centrally located and tastefully decorated. Full, hearty English breakfasts, full vegetarian. Close to seafront/town, all rooms offer en suite facilities.
Facilities:	P
To Beach:	0.28 miles

WHITBY – WEST CLIFF

Saxonville Hotel

★★Hotel

SILVER AWARD

Ladysmith Avenue, Whitby, YO21 3HX

T:	+44 (0) 1947 602631
E:	newtons@saxonville.co.uk
W:	saxonville.co.uk
Bedrooms:	23 • £113.00-£143.00 per double room per night, breakfast included • Debit/credit card accepted
Open:	Seasonal opening – call for details
Description:	Family-owned hotel, in operation since 1946, proud of its good food and friendly atmosphere. Non-smoking hotel.
Facilities:	
To Beach:	0.17 miles

WHITBY – WEST CLIFF

Seacliffe Hotel ★★★★Guest Accommodation

12 North Promenade, Whitby, YO21 3JX

T:	+44 (0) 1947 603139
E:	info@seacliffe.fsnet.co.uk
W:	seacliffe.co.uk
Bedrooms:	21 • £77.90-£87.90 per double room per night, breakfast included
Open:	Seasonal opening – call for details
Description:	Seacliffe is a small, friendly hotel with a restaurant offering a la carte menu. In a prime position on the seafront. Licensed, open all year, sea views. Ideal for the moors and coast.
Facilities:	
To Beach:	0.25 miles

WHITBY – WEST CLIFF

Wentworth House ★★★Guesthouse

27 Hudson Street, Whitby, YO21 3EP

T:	+44 (0) 1947 602433
E:	info@whitbywentworth.co.uk
W:	whitbywentworth.co.uk
Bedrooms:	6 • £52.00 per double room per night, breakfast included
Open:	Year round
Description:	Small, friendly, family-run B&B. Pets welcome. Central location for beach, town pubs, restaurant and all the facilities of the North York Coast and moors.
Facilities:	
To Beach:	0.22 miles

WHITBY – WEST CLIFF

White Linen Guesthouse ♦♦♦♦Guest Accommodation

24 Bagdale, Whitby, YO21 1QS

T:	+44 (0) 1947 603635
E:	info@whitelinenguesthouse.co.uk
W:	whitelinenguesthouse.co.uk
Bedrooms:	9 • £70.00-£90.00 per double room per night, breakfast included • Debit/credit card accepted
Open:	Seasonal opening – call for details
Description:	Family-run Georgian dwelling, located in the centre of historic Whitby. Beautifully renovated with elegant furnishings, offering all en suite bedrooms.
Facilities:	
To Beach:	0.48 miles